Move Up

Praise for

Move Up

"Coming up, I tried to do everything I could to study the industry and learn about the craft, and the best place to do that was always STAA. Jon has taken so much of what I pulled from and created a book that every young broadcaster must have. I just wish he had written this 15 years ago!"

Joe Davis
FOX Sports
Los Angeles Dodgers

"I found myself nodding several times, thinking, 'So true...that aligns exactly with my experience in broadcasting.' Jon's advice & expertise are a big reason I landed my first job out of college, setting me on my path to call games on national TV. This book will help everyone in the industry, from those just getting started to those who have spent decades in the business."

Connor Onion
ESPN

"This book is not only a guide to get started and continue to thrive in the sportscasting industry, but also includes relevant stories, funny analogies, and relatable situations that can make you better in any professional environment. No surprise, coming from someone who has made a career out of helping others improve themselves, including me."

Chris Lewis

CBS Sports

"I love Jon's advice about being an elite person (not just an elite announcer) and the astute connection he makes between personal growth and career growth. This book fills a void in the industry: it's both a roadmap and a point of reference for broadcasters at any stage of their journey. Jon's message—and sense of humor—resonates with me today as much as it did at the start of my career."

Chris Vosters

Big Ten Network

NBC Sports

"Jon's guidance helped shape my broadcasting career and this book carries that same clarity and insight. It's a smart, honest guide packed with real-world advice for standing out and advancing in the sports broadcasting industry."

Katie Storm

Fan Duel Sports Network North

"I literally owe my first job in the business to Jon as my employer found me on STAA. His passion for helping journalists and the excitement he had calling me about that gig was evident then and has never wavered in the 11 years I have known him. He's been a trusted ally in this space and one I am always grateful for."

Brenna Greene

KOIN TV, Portland, OR

"Jon Chelesnik is a sage in the world of sportscasting. He has had an immeasurable impact on my career, from NAIA basketball all the way to MLB. Jon has been a consistent source of advice, honest feedback, and kind guidance for me over the years. With this book, he now generously offers his wisdom to a wider audience who seek to navigate an ever-evolving sportscasting landscape."

Gary Hill

Seattle Mariners

"I truly believe Jon Chelesnik is the premier sports broadcasting mentor in the industry. A humble guide with an uncommon ability to impact lives, Jon has helped jumpstart hundreds of young careers. Throughout Move Up, you'll see his belief in relationship-building and paying it forward—principles he instilled in me from my days in the rugged Alaska Baseball League to my work with the Savannah Bananas and Westwood One. Jon has gifted the world a cheat code for advancing a sports broadcasting career."

Drake Toll

Westwood One Sports Radio

The Savannah Bananas

Move Up

Uncommon advice to advance your sportscasting career

JON CHELESNIK

Go Be Great Books
Del Mar, CA
2025

Go Be Great Books
Box 1024
Del Mar, CA 92014
jon@staatalent.com

ISBN 979-8-9939706-0-8 paperback
ISBN 979-8-9939706-1-5 ebook

Cover design by Ryan Chelesnik
Edited by Troy Powers and Amy Chelesnik

Published by STAA
Go Be Great Books, an imprint of STAA
Printed in the United States of America

First Edition

Manufactured in the United States of America
10 9 8 7 6 5 4 3 2 1

This book is dedicated to the thousands of people who have either been members of Sportscasters Talent Agency of America, referred folks to STAA, worked for us, or provided support and encouragement. I am grateful.

"The difference between a successful person and others is not a lack of strength, not a lack of knowledge, but rather a lack of will."

- Vince Lombardi

Table of Contents

FOREWARD

I started my broadcasting journey like Dory. Then I met Jon Chelesnik.

If you have seen the movie *Finding Nemo* you know that Dory attacks the day with endless enthusiasm. She "just keeps swimming." But where?

When I decided I wanted to be a sports broadcaster, I dove in head first, but had no idea where to start or what to aim for. Jon Chelesnik gave me the guardrails and the goals. He helped me find direction. Thanks to him, I learned how to swim in a straight line instead of in circles.

Jon has sat in a lot of the same chairs as you and me. His experience as a National ESPN Radio Host, a play-by-play broadcaster and a sideline reporter gave him a real feel for the industry. His 19+ years of studying and dissecting the industry through the lens of STAA gives him insight into the behind the scenes of the industry. He has lived it, studied it, and taught it. This truly unique perspective has helped me and many others find their way through the waters of the sports broadcasting industry.

When I arrived in college there were no classes or professors who taught play-by-play. Jon filled that void and became my lifelong professor. Through our conversations I've learned how to approach the job industry, what employers look for, and how to find my voice. I wondered how Jon always had answers to my millions of questions and how his advice was always practical. Then I realized what makes him such a good teacher. He never stops being a student. He'll ask as many questions as you do. Jon is open to talking about and challenging the rules of broadcasting and thrives in creative thinking when approaching the job market. As much as he teaches, he learns more.

This book is full of tools to help you grow. Jon will provide advice on how to keep swimming when you "feel stuck." He will challenge you to turn inward and reflect deeply on your own beliefs and processes. The information in this book encapsulates the invaluable lessons he has taught me and so many others. Whether your goal is just to improve your own individual performance on the mic or catch your big break, this book will help get you there.

I hope you decide to dive into this journey that is Jon's advice. If you are chasing a life of growth, this book is for you. By the end you'll come away sharper as a broadcaster and even pick up some skills that go beyond the job. If you are ready to be challenged, to find your next step and to swim with purpose, please read on.

Carlo Jiménez
Radio Play-by-Play Broadcaster
Los Angeles Clippers

Introduction

My sportscasting career flourished in July 2003, my 14th year in the industry. I was in my fourth year as a host on ESPN Radio Network, and was broadcasting for a startup company called The Football Network (TFN). I felt so good that one night at a local steakhouse with my wife, I ordered a large steak and a second salad—something I never previously thought I could afford.

July 2003 was the pinnacle of my on-air career and income. Five months later, I was out of the industry. ESPN let me go, and TFN folded.

No more extra salads.

Sitting down to consider my career options was scary. I was ready to try something different, but my skills and options were limited. I couldn't cook or change the oil in my car. Sportscasting was all I knew. After much consideration—and homemade hamburgers instead of restaurant steaks—I combined my knowledge of sportscasting with my love for helping people.

I began earning money creating demo and resume packages for sportscasters to help them stand out in the job market. It quickly became apparent they wanted help in other areas, too— finding job openings, writing cover letters, following up applications, building relationships, and many other things not taught in sportscasting school. My company, Sportscasters Talent Agency of America (STAA), was born to provide that guidance.

STAA's history includes a blog. It addresses the most common questions and concerns sportscasters share with me about how to move up. My advice is rooted in my experiences, those of other sportscasters, and insight from employers. The blog became this book, which includes amusing, inspiring, and real stories illustrating what to do and what not to do to advance your career.

You'll learn uncommon advice for moving to the next level, including strategies for:

- Setting yourself apart in a crowded industry
- Finding unpublicized job openings
- Getting replies to your applications
- Building relationships to advance your career
- Getting unstuck
- Navigating challenges when your career isn't unfolding as planned

This book is not about how to be a sportscaster but how to move up in your career. It is of great value to young sportscasters. It is even more valuable to veterans.

You can read the book cover-to-cover or use it like a grocery store, grabbing what you need when you need it. Either way, you'll get a brain dump of nearly 40 years of my light bulb moments to help you advance in your sportscasting career.

Work on your craft.

Work on yourself.

Go be great.

Chapter 1:

Career Advancement

Focus on the Job at Hand

An ambitious young sportscaster graduated from college and started a job at a small market radio station. The position had everything he could ask for in a first gig—tons of play-by-play, daily sports updates, and a full-time salary with benefits.

It was the perfect situation to hone his craft for the next two or three years. That's why I was stunned by the question he asked after less than one month in the position.

"Where do you think I should be looking for my next job?"

I almost fell out of my chair. I asked for clarification. "You're less than four weeks into an awesome job, yet you're already thinking about your next opportunity?"

Focus on the job at hand. Focusing on what's next prevents you from doing your best in your current position.

There are many ways to advance your sportscasting career–things like building relationships, distributing resumes, and attending conferences. However, **the best way to get your next job is to do your best in your current opportunity.**

When Mookie Betts was traded to the Dodgers in 2020 in the final year of his contract, he didn't worry about where he would be playing in 2021. Instead, he focused on the job at hand. The payoff was a 2020 World Series title and a monstrous new deal with LA.

You don't have to promote yourself for better opportunities when you consistently do great work. Others will do it for you, and opportunity will find you.

EXERCISE PATIENCE

Ten years out of college, I finally achieved my big break—hosting Weekend AllNight on ESPN Radio. Two years later, at age 34, I added play-by-play and sideline reporting duties for a national cable TV startup devoted exclusively to football (before even the NFL Network).

Vince Lombardi, arguably the greatest NFL coach in history, was coaching high school football at age 38.

There is no such thing as an overnight success. We'll talk more about that in the Professional Development chapter. The bottom line, though, is that most people invest years of hard work in anonymity before achieving renown.

Advancing your career slowly today can help you move faster tomorrow. An aspiring play-by-play broadcaster is better off honing their craft in Sheboygan than taking a job in Chicago where they aren't calling games.

Career progress often takes longer than desired because a person must gain experience and wisdom. Still, impatience is understandable and common in our industry.

A sportscaster sent this email to me:

"I feel like I'm ready to move up the ladder, but the fact is that I simply don't have that much experience yet. I'm just now entering my third year of post-graduate employment. Sometimes, it is frustrating to feel like I'm 'stuck' where I am for a few more years. That doesn't mean that I don't value the opportunity to work and do games where I do, but I'm sure it's frustrating for others as well who feel like they're ready but need more experience."

Does that resonate with you? When reading that email, two thoughts come to mind:

1. Our friend isn't stuck; he is growing.

Every day spent doing your best in your current job moves you a day closer to your dream job.

2. You don't decide when you are ready.

The job market makes that decision. When you're ready, you'll get hired.

Sports broadcasting usually takes roughly 10 years before a person earns a comfortable living.

The people who make it to the top are often not the most talented. They are the most patient.

MOVE UP WHEN GROWTH STOPS

My favorite Whitney Houston song is "How Will I Know." I had the cassette in college and listened to it often. I mention it because someone asked me, "How will I know when it's time to go to a major market?"

They wondered, "Is it better to be freelancing and looking for opportunities while living in my desired market, or should I stay where I am and tough it out while pursuing other opportunities?"

I lean towards moving to the market where you want to be because most employers prefer to hire locally. My first job was in McPherson, Kansas, but I always wanted to work at XTRA Sports 690 in my hometown of San Diego. I sent 10 cassettes over two years to the program director, Howard Freedman. I never heard back.

After three years in Kansas, I felt I had learned all I was going to in that job. I moved back to San Diego, figuring I needed to live there if I wanted to work there. I was right. Freedman hired me less than three months later. He said the fact I was now living locally was the difference.

My career flourished after I arrived.

It's time to move up when you feel no more room for growth. Just understand that your new job might start as part-time, and you'll have to find additional work to help pay the bills.

If you feel like a flower that's outgrown its pot, moving to a bigger market is the only way you'll grow.

LET THE JOB MARKET GUIDE YOU

Jamelle Holieway was the best option quarterback I have ever watched. It was must-see TV when he ran Oklahoma's wishbone attack in the 1980s. As I watched in awe, I wondered how Holieway chose to keep or pitch the ball on each play. In reality, the defense chose for him. If the end stays wide, keep it. If the end collapses, pitch it. Easy.

Planning your sportscasting career can be like running the option. For example, does an aspiring Major League Baseball broadcaster stick with the long days and low pay of Minor League ball or opt for the stability of being an NCAA Division I football and basketball voice?

How do you choose?

While working at XTRA Sports 690, my career options were play-by-play and sports talk host. I was doing both, but knew a choice would eventually have to be made. I didn't want to make it, though, so I applied for big-time gigs in both fields. That led me to ESPN Radio Network.

I didn't have to decide between sports talk and play-by-play. Nobody offered me a play-by-play role, so the job market chose for me.

As a job seeker, the job market is what the defensive end was to Jamelle Holieway: It will make your decision for you.

If you are torn between two sportscasting career paths, pursue them both. The market will decide where your value is greatest.

BALANCE CAREER, FINANCES, AND FAMILY

A sportscaster emailed to share he was facing one of the biggest challenges in his career. He asked, "How do I know what the right next step is for me? I know I'll be successful at higher levels, but I earn a great salary here, and I've set down roots."

Prioritize three considerations to determine your best next step: career, finances, and family.

1. Career

Study the paths of people who are already where you want to be. A handful of commonalities exists in how somebody goes from entry-level to a large market or network. Study those paths to determine what your reasonable next move might be.

Something to consider when planning your next step is how well your next employer can sell you to their audience. If you are applying to be the voice of the New York Yankees, yet all you've done is American Legion ball in McPherson, Kansas, it doesn't matter if you're the second coming of legendary Yankees radio voice John Sterling. It will be impossible for the Yankees to sell to their fans that their next voice was doing Legion ball in Kansas.

If your desired next employer won't be able to market you reasonably to their fan base, you're not ready for that step.

2. Finances

Financial considerations become increasingly important when you marry and possibly start a family. You can't always take the next job that's better for your career if it means you won't be able to support your family as comfortably as you do now.

Also, remember the cost of living varies across the country. San Francisco is one of the most expensive places in the U.S., but other top 20 markets are much more affordable. Use an online cost-of-living calculator to compare the value of a dollar where you live now to the city to which you might be moving.

3. Family

One of my sportscasting mentors told me when I was in college to stay single as long as possible. He said broadcasting's frequent moves and minimal pay weren't conducive to a good marriage. He added that marriage could limit my freedom to go where the jobs are.

Conversely, a supportive spouse is a wonderful benefit in our challenging profession.

Planning your next career move is entirely different when you are married, especially if you have kids. You are no longer making decisions unilaterally. You no longer have the freedom to go wherever you want. "What does this move do for my career?" becomes a secondary consideration.

Additional considerations for married sportscasters:

- Can I support my family on this income?
- What are the chances my spouse can find work in the new location?
- Is my spouse willing to live here?
- How happy is my spouse going to be?
- If my spouse compromises on my behalf, might it lead to resentment?
- What will be the emotional impact on my kids to leave their school and friends?

I was lucky. At different times during my sportscasting career, my wife and I faced the prospect of moving from San Diego to places like Boston, Little Rock, and Baton Rouge. My wife was always on board with wherever we might have to go. Not all sportscasters have such unwavering support, but I wish it for everyone.

My advice to married sportscasters who are considering a move is this:

Give equal or more weight to your spouse's desires. You can't put a price on happiness. A good marriage is even more fulfilling than a solid career.

CREATE A PLAN

Growing up in San Diego, I am a long-suffering Padres fan. The highlight of my fandom was 1984. I was at the old Jack Murphy Stadium when the Friars beat the Cubs in the deciding game of the NLCS to move on to the World Series.

One of my all-time favorite Padres was closer Kirby Yates. He went from being released by the Angels to an All-Star in San Diego. He did it by having a plan: stay in shape and develop a new pitch—the splitter.

Like Kirby Yates, you should **create a plan for moving to the next level in your sports broadcasting career**. Here are three suggestions:

1. Always be building relationships.

It's sometimes hard to be motivated for relationship building because the payoff isn't immediate. Our industry is small, though. The people you meet and build relationships with today can help you advance your career tomorrow. Always be building relationships.

One key to creating strong relationships is not to approach people asking what they can do for you. Instead, offer something you can do for them. Offer to connect someone with a person who can help them, or volunteer to serve as a spotter for a play-by-play broadcaster. That is why we call this "relationship building" instead of networking. It's giving versus asking for something.

A second key: don't wait until you need water before digging your well. **Build relationships now so they're ready when you need them.**

2. Always be improving yourself.

It's even more important to work on yourself than on your career. **Your income will directly relate to the effort you put into self-improvement.** Always be improving yourself.

Later in this book is a chapter titled Personal Growth. For now, I'll share three books that have helped me a ton:

- *Think And Grow Rich*, by Napoleon Hill. It's been around for almost 100 years.
- *See You At The Top* by Zig Ziglar. Another classic.
- *The Secret* by Rhonda Byrne. A life changer for me.

Wherever you find inspiration, constantly improve yourself. It will make it much easier to move to the next level in your sportscasting career.

3. Always be improving your craft.

Self-critiquing, requesting critiques from others, and studying other sportscasters ensure you are always getting better.

A ship doesn't leave the harbor without plotting a course for its destination. Similarly, having a plan will help you get where you want to go in your career.

START LOOKING IMMEDIATELY WHEN LIFE FORCES A MOVE

A sportscaster I know is stressed. His wife is the family's primary breadwinner. She has accepted a position forcing their family to move to another state. His anxiety stems from having no sportscasting work lined up in their new city.

Another broadcaster friend of mine moved back to his hometown to help his aging parents.

How do you handle being forced to leave your job and move to a place where nothing awaits you professionally?

There are two reasons why finding work might be easier than you think:

1. You'll be able to introduce yourself to potential new employers in person.

If you know you will move soon, contact employers in your new market now. Can you schedule a time to introduce yourself briefly? Don't ask for a job—just for an introduction.

2. You'll be available to fill in at a moment's notice.

Being available for emergency fill-in immediately makes you valuable to an employer and allows you to demonstrate your worth.

Finding work in a new market might take several months. **Starting your search before you move increases the chance you will hit the ground running.**

Tell your boss you're leaving only when it's time

How do you think it would go over if you told your significant other that you are starting to look for someone new? At the least, it would likely put a strain on the relationship. In the worst case, your significant other tells you to get lost.

It's the same in the job market. **The best time to tell your boss you're looking elsewhere is when you've accepted another job.** There is one exception that I will address in a moment.

If you tell your employer you are looking at other opportunities, you risk four things happening–none of them good.

1. Creating animosity

Some employers will take your search personally. Instead of understanding that you are trying to further your career, they believe your interest in new opportunities indicates you don't like working for them. Or they feel you are being disloyal after they gave you a job.

2. Getting fired

I have seen several times when an employer learned an employee was looking elsewhere and got rid of the person. I even saw it once at a national network. The thought is, "If you don't want to be here, we don't want you here."

3. Unfair speculation

A boss may wonder how much effort they are getting from an employee who already has one foot out the door.

4. Devaluing yourself

It might not look good on you if you tell your boss you are starting to look elsewhere, then your search takes a long time. Your value drops in the eyes of your employer when nobody else is hiring you. At that point, good luck getting a raise out of them.

One option is to tell your boss you're looking elsewhere when another company invites you to interview. Only do this, though, if you have an excellent relationship with your boss. For example, many minor league baseball general managers understand their broadcasters want to be upwardly mobile. Some even want to help their announcers move up the ladder because they like the individual, and it reflects well on the organization when their people are in demand. In such cases, you can feel comfortable telling your boss you have an interview elsewhere.

Mostly, what your boss doesn't know won't hurt them. Or you.

Resign the Right Way

When you resign from a job, you can burn a bridge or build a relationship.

Understand this about resigning: *When you give your notice, your boss might immediately take you off the air.* Some bosses are paranoid about a departing talent saying bad things about the station on the air. Sounds unreasonable, I know, but it happens.

The wrong way to tell your boss you are leaving is not giving sufficient notice. Without it, you put your boss on the spot to find your replacement quickly.

Also, be sure not to express frustration about your employment or unusual joy that you are leaving. It makes you look immature and unprofessional; neither is desirable. Plus, sportscasting is a small industry. Stories of unprofessional behavior have a knack for traveling. Expressing frustration or joy about leaving might feel good, but you may unknowingly be removing yourself from consideration for future opportunities elsewhere.

Here are four things you can do when resigning that your boss will appreciate:

1. Give at least two weeks written notice.

Your leaving will likely create stress for your boss. They must write a position description, publicize it, review dozens of demos and resumes, and interview candidates before hiring your replacement. Two weeks' notice gives them reasonable time.

Writing your resignation and handing it to your boss is best. Doing so eliminates potential ambiguity about when you gave notice and your last day of availability.

2. Suggest candidates to replace you.

Offering potential replacements also helps relieve some of the stress you've placed on your boss with your pending departure.

3. Say thank you.

You felt fired up about this position when hired because it was a great opportunity at that point in your career. Let your boss know you appreciate the chance they gave you.

4. Help your successor.

Make the transition easier for your successor by leaving a written document detailing the various aspects of the job and how to execute them.

Be classy, even if you don't honestly like where you are leaving. It is the professional thing to do. And if done with compassion and appreciation, it can ensure that your ex-boss is a friend instead of a foe.

HEAL YOUR CONFIDENCE AFTER BEING FIRED

The most discouraging phone call of my career was in July 2003. I took it while sitting at the desk in my home office in Carlsbad, CA. ESPN Radio Network was replacing me after four years of hosting Weekend AllNight. I felt shock, disbelief, anger, despair, betrayal, bewilderment, and a loss of confidence. Maybe I wasn't as good as I thought. Otherwise, they wouldn't be replacing me, right?

I was 36. I sobbed.

After several days, I could sort through most of my emotions. The one that remained, though, was my lack of confidence. I wondered if I had been fooling management for the past four years. Maybe they never listened to the show. After all, it aired in the middle of the night on weekends. Perhaps when they finally listened, they realized it sucked. Or the person who hired me thought of weekend overnights as a throwaway shift. When new management came in, I reasoned, they put new emphasis on the time slot and thought I wasn't good enough.

In the years since, I've learned that losing confidence often follows losing a job. Fortunately, there are things you can do to help yourself.

1. Understand the reason for your dismissal might have nothing to do with performance.

Management may want someone more affordable. Perhaps new management wants to bring in their "own guy." Maybe somebody doesn't like you. Whatever the reason, getting fired doesn't automatically mean you're not good.

2. Understand that sportscasting is like coaching.

Sportscasters and coaches are hired to be fired. The number of major market sportscasters who have been fired is staggering. Realizing that it happens to almost everyone makes it easier to appreciate there isn't something uniquely wrong with you. Getting fired ends your job, not your career.

3. Know that losing a job often leads to a better position. Read on.

GETTING FIRED CAN BE GREAT

In 2003, wildfires raged throughout much of where I live in Southern California. I'll never forget flying into the airport and seeing thousands of acres of red-orange flames and billowing black smoke stretching its fingers toward the airplane. The land looked hopeless as if nothing would ever grow there again.

Today, that ground is full of young, strong, beautiful trees, colorful wildflowers, and sagebrush. The land flourished following the disaster.

Getting fired in sports broadcasting can be similar. I have seen countless broadcasters build their careers upon getting fired—always taking a step forward after what looked like a step back.

Don't despair if you lose your job.

Things were going great for a friend through his first year at a radio station. Then, they suddenly eliminated his position. He and his wife had just had a baby. Now, he was unemployed. He was beside himself with despair.

My friend allowed himself one day of pity, then hit the job market. He landed a position six weeks later in a much larger market at twice his previous salary.

He flourished following a disaster.

Nobody wants to be fired. If it happens, embrace the chance that it might move you forward.

Get Back in the Game After Being Fired

In September 2014, The Beast 980 went on the air in Los Angeles. A second ownership group bought the station 16 months later and dropped the sports format.

That sucked. It sucked for Tom Lee, who had moved to LA just 10 months before to take over as program director. It sucked for Jeanne Zelasko and Bill Plaschke, who had started their new morning show only three months earlier. It sucked for Chris Myers and Wes Clements, who began hosting an afternoon show just one month earlier. It sucked for Fred Roggin, who moved to Afternoon Drive three months earlier. It sucked for Sam Farber, who had just become the Clippers radio network host that season. It sucked for Pete Arbogast, whose AM sports anchoring schedule fit nicely around his gig as the voice of USC Trojans football. It sucked for everyone who lost their job, whether they were on or off the air.

The great news? All but one of them continued in sportscasting. Sam Farber even later became the radio voice for the Charlotte Hornets.

Use the following steps as your game plan to get back on the air:

1. Grieve and re-group.

Does it sound silly to grieve a job? Even if you suspected it was coming, losing a job is a blow. The more you enjoyed and invested in the job, the more it hurts. As with any shock, give yourself time to process before diving back into the job market. Take a day or two. Spend extra time with your family and friends, see a movie, or enjoy a hobby.

2. Limit complaining.

Losing a job for any reason is always a knock to your pride. If your situation ends badly, you might feel tempted to vent to a colleague or even on social media. Words spoken in anger to the wrong person may haunt you, though. Keep your complaints within a limited circle—people you can trust to handle your gut reactions with discretion.

3. Choose a positive attitude.

Do your best not to take being fired personally. Negative emotions and attitudes can unknowingly color your job search. Employers don't want to hire your baggage. And, as previously alluded to, being fired might turn out for the better. Losing a job can help you realize how much you've grown, how much you have to offer a new employer, and how much more your experience and ability are worth in the market.

4. Tell everyone.

Hopefully, you've been building good relationships throughout your career. It's time to put them to use! If people don't know you've lost your job, they can't help you find your next one. Don't assume a person has already heard your news. Even if they have, they might presume you have another gig lined up or may not realize you are actively looking.

Make your contacts via phone and email—phone for your closest relationships; email for the rest. Avoid blasting a form letter to everyone in your email contacts. Resist the urge to save time or avoid uncomfortable conversations about what happened. You built personal relationships. Making individual contacts deepens those relationships and will yield better results.

Also, don't get in touch to ask for a job. Instead, ask for advice. Sometimes, when you ask for advice, you get a job. Ask your industry friends to send your contact info to employers if they know of a potential opening.

Your contact message should be as simple as a couple of sentences:

Hey NAME,

I want to let you know that I'm no longer with PREVIOUS EMPLOYER. I'm not asking for a job—I know you already have a great broadcast team, and I respect their work. If you hear of any potential [JOB TYPE] openings, though, please let me know.

Thank you!

5. Use social media.

Activating your social media followers is a great way to cast a wider net. Don't be shy to let folks know you are eagerly searching for your next opportunity. There are people following you who appreciate your work and might be in a position to help you find a new job.

6. Use the referral request technique.

The referral request is a great way to uncover job leads and build connections. The goal is to connect with people—not to seek immediate employment, but to build a network that could lead to referrals.

Instructions for executing the referral request are in the Chapter 2: Job Market section, *Prompt People to Recommend Opportunities.*

7. Keep a calendar.

Have a calendar you use only for your job market pursuits. Schedule who you will contact and when. Also schedule follow-ups with those folks every six weeks or so.

8. Target your value regions.

Identify the regions where you're most marketable: your current city, hometown, and college town. These are what I call your value regions.

Make a list of people you know in each region. Who is important to contact immediately? Is there anyone with insight into what you might have done differently in your last job? Could someone help you brainstorm ideas for your next job? Make a second list of employers that you want to cold contact.

9. Stay busy

Looking for a full-time job IS a full-time job. Write down 10 things you will do each day to move toward your next opportunity. Staying busy and proactive in the job market will help you keep a positive mindset. Here's a to-do list to get you started:

- Update your demo, resume, website, and the profile image on your social media (get a new headshot if you need one)
- Don't have a website? Build one!
- Reach out to contacts in your value regions and cold-contact list (Read about cold contacting in Chapter 2)
- Brainstorm three creative ways to follow up your applications (Read about following up in Chapter 2).
- Look for freelance opportunities
- Publish a note on social media thanking your audience

You might also volunteer somewhere. Helping others is guaranteed to help you feel good about yourself.

10. Stay relevant

We often intend to improve skills in areas where we are weak, but the day-to-day grind gets in the way. Have you been meaning to improve your graphic design skills? Learn how to edit video? Up your social media game?

Use your newly freed time to learn a new skill or sport. The time between jobs is the perfect opportunity to try new things and ensure you are a well-rounded broadcaster.

Losing a job isn't an end. It's the beginning of the next step in your career. Take a day for self-pity, then start looking at the loss of your job as the birth of a new opportunity. Getting fired doesn't happen4 to you; it happens for you. Knowing that will help you land your next opportunity; maybe a better one.

FIVE WAYS TO POSITION AGE AS AN ADVANTAGE

"ESPN and Fox are hiring much younger these days."

A long-time play-by-play broadcaster shared that frustration with me. Another veteran struggling to find work laments that sportscasting "is a young man's game now."

For these sportscasters in their late 40s to early 50s, age has become the biggest challenge to career advancement. "Being cast as an 'old school' broadcaster is probably a detriment," says one of them.

The perception that it is harder for older sportscasters to find work is accurate. However, understanding employers' trepidation about hiring older voices can help you present yourself better in the job market.

Here are five challenges faced by older sportscasting job seekers and how to spin them as positives in your cover letter:

1. Veteran sportscasters cost more money.

Be willing to work for less than what you are used to. Tell employers you understand how compensation has changed over the years and that you are eager to work for the amount budgeted for the position.

2. Up-and-comers bring more enthusiasm, hunger, and motivation.

"My work ethic is born of years of perfecting my craft and love for [my particular sport). My passion for my career has never been greater because I now have the experience and knowledge to match my motivation."

3. Younger broadcasters often don't have wives and children pulling them from the job.

I have a wife and children and want to set down roots. Your job is a destination for me, not a stepping stone.

4. The big fish in the small pond will eventually become disgruntled.

I have worked at [higher levels] of the industry. Now, fulfillment for me would come from contributing to a successful organization.

5. Pro teams and universities want guys who are going to be there for 20 years.

Include a brief list of sportscasters still going strong into their 70s.

You certainly bring other positives to the table that younger sportscasters cannot. Think about them and sell them in your cover letter.

Implementing these tips won't guarantee work, but it will undoubtedly give you a better shot.

Chapter 2:

Job Market

DEMOS

CHOOSE FROM YOUR MOST RECENT WORK

The play-by-play gig at the University of Kentucky opened two years into my first radio job in McPherson, Kansas. The legendary Cawood Ledford had passed away. I naively thought I could go from calling the Mac High Bullpups to the Kentucky Wildcats.

I spent 20 hours trying to find the best stuff for my demo. What a waste of time.

Save yourself from the same mistake. **Choose from your most recent work.**

Your latest work represents where you are in your development, for better or worse.

If you are a play-by-play broadcaster, you either state the time and score consistently or don't. You pinpoint the ball consistently, or you don't. If you don't do it in your most recent work, you likely weren't doing it three months earlier.

Similarly, a sports talk host is having opinions, making topics relatable, and telling stories, or they aren't.

When building that demo for UK, I reviewed football and basketball broadcasts from the two most recent seasons, looking for what I thought belonged on the demo. Great action. No stumbles. Clever phrasing. Segments that sounded smooth—where I didn't get so confused or fall so far behind the action that there were odd pauses while I was trying to figure things out.

It turns out none of that is what employers were listening for.

STAA's Play-by-Play and Sports Talk Pyramids outline what employers want to hear. You will find them in the appendix at the back of this book.

You should improve with every broadcast. **Your latest broadcast should be your best**, and your best is what should be on your demo.

MAKE IT "REPRESENTATIVE OF" VS. "BEST OF"

Employers don't want to hear your "best of." They want to listen to what you do every day.

Among my favorite sportscasters was Ted Leitner, the longtime former voice for my hometown Padres and San Diego State. I also very much enjoy Jim Rome and Dan Patrick. Any segment of their broadcasts is indicative of their ability and style. I didn't have to hear Leitner call a walk-off home run to know he is good. Anyone can make that sound exciting. What made Leitner great was his ability to be entertaining in the fifth inning of a 4-to-1 game.

Same thing for sports talk hosts. The easiest day of the year to host a show is the day after the Super Bowl. Don't put that on your demo. The Mount Rushmore of pitchers? Same thing. It's low-hanging fruit. Instead, use something that shows you can be entertaining and different on more challenging topics.

Basketball coaches don't judge players based on the few occasions when that player is "in the zone." Instead, they write their scouting reports around what that player does the other times.

Your demo is your scouting report about yourself.

Ensure that what you send to employers represents the "every day you."

START FAST

Motown Records is one of history's most successful and influential record-producing companies. It reached its peak in the 1960s and 70s.

What was unique about much of Motown's songwriting was that it started fast. It grabbed you right off the bat.

The song "Get Ready" by the Temptations begins with a bold horns riff. Marvin Gaye's classic song "What's Going On" starts with nightclub chatter. You think, "What's this? I've never heard this in a song before." It grabs your attention. Another Temptations song, "Ain't Too Proud to Beg," starts with David Ruffin wailing painfully in his signature scratchy voice, "I know you want to leave me."

Motown Records made gazillions from starting songs with a hook—something powerful and memorable. They didn't start at zero and then slowly accelerate to sixty. Instead, they started many of their songs at sixty. They produced the musical equivalent of a splash of cold water on your face.

Apply the same "start fast" strategy to your demo.

Begin each play-by-play demo with one minute of highlights. Start a sports anchoring and reporting demo with an energetic, great line or unique camera shot. For sports talk hosting, open with a story or attention-grabbing statement.

Start your sports demo with a hook. Get employers fired up, curious, and excited for what comes next.

60 seconds is enough; no more than 90. Too much ice cream is a bad thing.

LESS IS MORE

A sports radio program director in a major market received a link to a website from a job applicant. The site featured a half dozen sports talk samples. The employer told him, "I haven't listened to the amount of tape you have posted, even for the most important hires of my career. I can decide in five seconds if I will give you one more minute of my time."

A sportscaster invited me to listen to a demo on his website. He pointed me to a specific basketball play-by-play track. It was one of several on the page.

If you have a great sample you want to be sure an employer reviews, make it the only sample of that genre—for example, basketball play-by-play.

Less is more. **A good demo features quality tracks over quantity.**

Before sending several demo links to an employer, ask yourself, "If you have someone's attention for five seconds, what do you most want them to hear?" Share your best and favorite work.

Again, less is more.

Keep it Fresh

There is a common demo reel mistake that can kill your big break when it finally comes your way. Here is the first-hand account from the person it happened to:

"I can't stress enough how stupid I feel for not regularly updating my reels.

"I recently was at Mohegan Sun (a casino/resort in Connecticut). I was playing blackjack at a table with someone who works in the video production department for BU Athletics. We got to talking; I mentioned I do broadcasting; we swapped numbers and emails so we could talk further about me doing work for them this year. The following week, I had an email in my inbox asking for my reels so he could get a sense of my previous work.

"I didn't have them ready.

"I had to send him an email with links to YouTube highlight packages, saying I'd follow up with more extensive samples as soon as I could. Man, did I feel embarrassed. It's possible I shot myself in the foot and lost the opportunity to leverage the connection I made. If that's the case, I will have no one but myself to blame, but I'll have learned a valuable lesson.

"It was a much-needed kick in the pants to get those reels updated/assembled and keep them fresh. And I can guarantee it's a lesson I won't soon forget."

I will add just one thing. The material on your demo reels should be updated at least annually.

You never know when you'll make a connection. Always be prepared.

RESUMES

ADD RIZZ AND SWAG—STRATEGICALLY

Let's get this out of the way now: my son will tell me I'm too old to say things like rizz, drip, and swag. He'd better get used to it because I'll use them again later. Hi Ryan!

Now, back to the action.

You only get one chance to make a great first impression in the sportscasting job market. A sharp resume and cover letter are how you'll make a great one. Give your resume personality and swag.

1. Rizz (charisma, personality)

Include more than just your work experience. Help employers get to know you; give them a chance to bond with you over shared interests. Things like Fun Facts and Favorites sections are great ways to do this. It's cool for an employer to know you were your school's 7th-grade long jump champ and you enjoy tacos and Friday Night Lights reruns.

2. Swag

LeBron James is one of the NBA's best-ever players and one of its all-time best-dressed performers. King James stands out wearing oversized shades, a shortsuit, and custom leather shoes in a room full of sneakers and jeans. LeBron has drip. He has swag.

Make yourself memorable by giving your resume rizz and swag. Sportscasting is an entertainment industry. Your resume should demonstrate your ability to stand out. **Pictures, colors, and graphics ensure your resume drips** like the following examples.

JOHN DOE

San Diego, CA
(619) 555-7822
name@gmail.com

ONLINE

Website:
staatalent.com

Facebook:
handle

Instagram:
handle

Twitter:
handle

LinkedIn:
handle

EDUCATION

B.A. Radio/Television
San Diego State University

X FACTOR

BOOK READER HOOPS PLAYER LAST CHANCE U FAN BEACH GOER HUSBAND DAD JOHN WOODEN FAN EXERCISER CHOCOLATE EATER COBRA KAI WATCHER

FAVORITES

Book: Ball Four by Jim Bouton
Movie: Rudy
Band: The Doors

What I Do . . .

SPORTS TALK

- ESPN Radio Network
- XTRA Sports 690
- San Diego Chargers Radio Network Host
- Jim Rome Show (fill-in), Sporting News Radio Network (fill-in)

PLAY-BY-PLAY

- Anaheim Piranhas, Arena Football League
- San Diego Stingrays, International Basketball League
- Kansas State University women's basketball
- Bethany College, KS football, men's & women's basketball
- McPherson College, KS football, men's & women's basketball
- High school football, basketball, baseball

ADDITIONAL RADIO

- San Diego Chargers Radio Network post-game locker room reporter

TELEVISION

- College football play-by-play, sideline reporting, TFN
- Analyst, International Basketball League
- Play-by-play for high school football, basketball

Where I've Done It . . .

- ESPN Radio, Bristol, CT, 1999 – 2003
- The Football Network, Los Angeles, CA, 1998 - 2003
- XTRA Sports 690, San Diego, CA, 1993 - 2000
- KNGL-KBBE, McPherson, KS, 1989 - 1993

Additional Skills . . .

Graphic Design ★★★★★
InDesign, Illustrator, Photoshop

Video ★★★★☆
Final Cut Pro, Avid, ENPS, EDIUS, Adobe Premier Pro, After Effects

CMS ★★★★☆
Word Press

Audio ★★★★★
Adobe Audition, Audacity

CONTACT

555-0199
shawn@email.com
St. Paul, Minnesota

SOCIAL MEDIA

@maineventvoice

Instagram

@maineventvoice

facebook

@maineventvoice

LinkedIn

@shawnwilliamparker

EDUCATION

University of Maryland, College Park

B.A., Broadcast Journalism, 2005

REFERENCES

Chadwick Folkstad, Arizona Coyotes
555-0199

Toby Stanga, Town Square Television
555-0199

Clinton Marsden, Mediacom
555-0199

EXPERIENCE

PUBLIC ADDRESS ANNOUNCER
Minnesota Timberwolves | 2017 – Present

- Player introductions, in-game announcements, player honors, sponsor reads and acknowledgements.

PLAY-BY-PLAY ANNOUNCER
Mediacom Communications | 2019 – Present

- Play-by-play for Minnesota Independent Wrestling and high school sporting events in the Minneapolis-St. Paul metro area.

PLAY-BY-PLAY ANNOUNCER
Town Square Television | 2018 – Present

- Play-by-play for Minnesota Vixen football and high school sporting events in the Inver Grove Heights area.

RADIO HOST
36 Nation | 2017

- Created, prepared, and presented up to date topics for live radio broadcast.
- Communicated with radio listeners via email, phone, and social media.
- Conducted on-air interviews on various topics.
- Develop online marketing strategies for sponsors and advertisers.

PUBLIC ADDRESS ANNOUNCER
George Washington University | 2014 – 2017

- Player introductions, in-game announcements, player honors, sponsor reads and acknowledgements.

PLAY-BY-PLAY ANNOUNCER
Gameday Broadcast Network/NFHS Network | 2015 – 2017

- Play-by-play for high school sporting events in the Washington, D.C. metro area.

Experience

BUCKEYE CABLE SPORTS NETWORK, OHIO

January 2013 – Currently

On-air talent, play-by-play broadcaster, sideline reporter

Local TV sports network broadcasting sports Ranging from high school to professional

SPEED SPORT TV, NORTH CAROLINA

August 2021 – Currently

Pit-reporter/Field producer

Lining up and executing interviews with drivers and teams during broadcast to share their stories

WESTERN OHIO SPORTS NETWORK, OHIO

December 2019 – Currently

Play-by-play broadcaster

Local TV sports network broadcasting high school sports across Western Ohio

MASON MITCHELL MOTORSPORTS, NORTH CAROLINA

August 2013 – July 2018

Public relations representative

write and distribute press releases. Work with sponsors to create brand presence. Create original content for all social media channels

AUTOMOBILE RACING CLUB OF AMERICA, MICHIGAN

May 2012 – October 2016

Play-by-play broadcaster

Radio broadcasts for the ARCA Racing Network and co-hosting weekly radio show

Education

BA Radio/TV Sports Broadcasting

Bowling Green State University

About Me

Dog lover
Vinyl collector
Pitmaster
Avid gardener

Favorites

Book: Greenlights by Matthew Mcconaughey
Movie: Friday Night Lights
Band: Tom Petty and The Heartbreakers

SKILLS

Video Editing (8/10)
●●●●●●●●○○

Audio (9/10)
●●●●●●●●●○

Filming (9/10)
●●●●●●●●●○

Microsoft Office Suite (8/10)
●●●●●●●●○○

Writing (9/10)
●●●●●●●●●○

References upon request

17 MORE FEATURES OF AWESOME RESUMES

Once your resume has rizz and swag, these suggestions will ensure it effectively communicates your experience—that its substance matches its style.

1. Make it one page.

Multi-page resumes are the norm in some industries. Sportscasting isn't one of them. The duties in our sector are simple enough not to require a detailed explanation. The pages of multi-page resumes are easily separated and can erroneously give an employer the impression you can't separate what's essential from what's not. An employer might have anywhere from 50 to 250 resumes to review. The longer your resume, the less time it will get. Ensure you don't lose the most important facts among the clutter.

2. Apply the Ten-Year Rule.

Employers don't care what you did more than a decade ago. You are a different person and broadcaster today. If space is becoming limited on your resume, delete experiences that are more than 10 years old.

3. Stay relevant.

Your resume should feature your sports broadcasting pursuits, not everything you've ever done. If you're young and the only job you've ever had was making sandwiches, it warrants a single sentence in an Additional Information section, at most.

4. Limit stylized text.

The purpose of stylized fonts is to make the most important facts stand out. When overused, though, nothing stands out. You should use stylized fonts only for your name and section headings. Larger font sizes, ALL CAPS, and italics are effective for section categories.

Avoid underlining on your resume. It looks cluttered, and some folks think it is supposed to be a clickable link.

5. Use bullet points.

Broadcasting isn't brain surgery and doesn't require a detailed explanation. A play-by-play broadcaster doesn't need to state they provide descriptions. We know. That is part of the job for any play-by-play broadcaster. Including it would be as redundant as a quarterback stating that he hands off to running backs and throws to receivers. Don't waste valuable space telling employers what they already know.

6. Embrace white space.

White space is easy on the eyes and keeps your resume from being overwhelming. Use reasonable margins on all four sides and between sections.

7. Emphasize your name.

Your name is the most essential information on the resume. Make it the largest font on the page so it stands out.

8. Include your URL.

Include your website in the header. Doing so pays dividends for online applications that don't offer a place to upload your demo.

9. Delete your street address.

Street addresses on resumes are old school. Employers conduct today's job market electronically. If employers want to send written correspondence to you, it will be via email. DO list your city and state in the header. Employers want to know where you are.

10. Don't label your phone and email.

People know what a phone number and email address are when they see them. Be lean.

11. Delete the objective.

Objectives are space-wasters. Employers assume your objective is to get the job you are applying for. Also, as you gain more experience, you'll want that additional space on the page.

12. Delete the summary.

Your resume IS a summary. There is no need to summarize the summary.

13. List your experience first.

After your name, your experience is the most important thing on the resume. Put that section first.

14. Emphasize sales experience.

Sales experience, if you have it, is one area of your resume where some detail is helpful. What did you sell, and how much? Include dollar figures to support an impressive sales history.

15. Chose references wisely.

If you include references, choose three and make them count. Industry references are best. Sportscasting is a small industry. If a potential employer knows one of your references, it can boost your candidacy.

Make sure your references are people whose names or titles carry credibility with employers. Athletic directors and coaches, even at prominent universities, carry minimal weight with broadcasting employers. While they can testify to your professionalism and character, they are not experts in sports broadcasting and cannot vouch for your on-air ability. It is the same with law enforcement officials, clergy members, and next-door neighbors. Employers want to hear from professionals who can attest to your ability to do the job.

For broadcasters just coming out of college who might not yet have three industry references, list a professor from your school's journalism department.

If you have a big name among your resume references—for example, an NFL or NBA play-by-play broadcaster or national sports talk host—include a personal phone number for that person. Listing a main office number leads some employers to question the strength of your relationship with the reference. There is also a strong chance a receptionist, trained to screen calls to high-profile personnel carefully, won't let your prospective employer's message through.

Finally, be certain to ask for permission to list each of your references on your resume. An employer once called to ask me about an applicant who used me as a reference without asking. I truthfully told the employer I didn't know the person well enough to provide a referral. I added that the person hadn't asked if he could use me as a reference. Another time, when someone didn't ask for permission to use me as a reference, I told the employer that the applicant wasn't qualified for the position.

16. Exclude reference email addresses.

If an employer wants to contact one of your references, they will call them. Including email addresses only clutters the page.

17. Always be evolving.

What is important on your resume today won't necessarily be tomorrow. It's like your spleen. Once upon a time, your spleen served an essential purpose. Through evolution, though, it no longer does. Internships are a resume spleen. They are helpful on your resume when first coming out of college, but real-world experience quickly trumps their value.

A fancy sports car looks cool in your driveway. If it doesn't have an engine, though, it won't get you where you want to go. Your sportscasting resume is similar. Looking good is impressive, but not enough. Be sure there is power under the hood.

AVOID CONFUSING EXPERIENCE WITH CREDIBILITY

Years ago, I played a pickup basketball game with former NBA player, coach, and general manager Danny Ainge. Sharing a court with Ainge didn't mean I was an NBA-caliber player. As the following 60 minutes proved, it meant only that I was a crummy player who happened to play a pickup game with an ex-NBA star.

Similarly, a common mistake sportscasters make on their resumes is inferring credibility based on a singular experience. Broadcasting a high school state championship game means the team was excellent. It doesn't mean the broadcaster was, too. Similarly, just because a person interviewed Patrick Mahomes doesn't make the person a great interviewer.

Sports broadcasting credibility doesn't result from the events and people you cover.

Credibility comes from ability.

Here are examples of irrelevant content from one person's resume:

- Participated in a press conference with Kevin Durant.
- Broadcasted the Women's Big Ten Championship.
- Covered two Bulls games and Women's Big Ten Media Day.
- Covered the announcement of the College Football Hall of Fame Class of 2024.

These experiences didn't make this sportscaster great by osmosis. Even after those events, this individual was still raw and inexperienced. Their resume would be stronger by deleting those bullet points and placing greater emphasis on practical experiences that are truly valuable.

Here's the fun finish to my Ainge story—I was hosting WeekendAllNight on ESPN Radio when we played that pickup game. After we finished, I asked Ainge to record a scouting report about me that I could use on the air. In short, he said, "Decent rebounder but otherwise has no game."

That covers the advice for resumes. A resume rubric is in the appendix of this book. It will show you if your resume is helping or hurting you in the sportscasting job market.

COVER LETTERS

EMBRACE THE ENTIRE POSITION DESCRIPTION

Did your mom say you can't have dessert if you don't eat your vegetables? My wife and I said it to our son all the time. You can't eat just the steak and garlic bread; you must also eat the peas.

It's the same when applying for jobs. You can't pretend the stuff you don't like in the position description doesn't exist.

I received an email from a small market radio station owner hiring for a position that combined sports and other duties. Many applicants killed their chances before the owner finished reading their cover letters.

Hear the frustration in what the station owner shared with me:

"If there is one common error these guys make—at least for a small market where you will be asked to do a variety of chores—they talk exclusively about their passion for sports and how much they know about the NBA, or the NFL, etc.

"We only care about our local high school—our sports guy will NEVER talk about the NBA.

"I need someone to do a board shift and talk about the local Girl Scouts. Some of these guys could do that, get some sports and play-by-play experience, and move up. But I now mark ASATT next to their name. It stands for ALL SPORTS ALL THE TIME...and if that's what they're about, I don't want them."

Another employer was hiring for a news/sports position. The job description emphasized the news part of the position. However, the employer told me applicants barely referenced the news part of the job in their cover letters, if they mentioned it at all!

Those people were immediately eliminated from consideration.

There are multiple lessons here:

1. Employer's priorities trump yours.

The sports part of a position may be the most interesting aspect to you, but that may not be the case for the employer. Job applications are not about what the employer can do for you and your career. They are about your ability to fill the employer's needs.

2. Write your letter to fit the position description.

If the description emphasizes news before mentioning sports, then emphasize your news experience in your cover letter before mentioning sports. Demonstrate your ability to be a good employee by showing you can identify the priorities of your potential future employer.

3. Apply only for jobs for which you are qualified.

Applying for jobs for which a person doesn't have the required skills and experience makes an applicant look ignorant while annoying the employer by wasting their time. Remember when I told you I applied for the University of Kentucky play-by-play job when I was working in McPherson, KS? I wasted their time. I wasn't qualified.

To re-emphasize: **When applying for a job, don't acknowledge in your cover letter only the parts of the position description you like.** Instead, declare your understanding and ability to do all of it.

Having a job is like finding a spouse. There's no such thing as the perfect one. If you can find a job or spouse that offers much more of what you like than what you don't, your chance to thrive is strong.

Customize for Each Position

I've received applications for dozens of major college play-by-play openings, sometimes several in one summer. People commonly send the same letter for multiple jobs within several days, changing only the school name. Applicants even fail to change the school's name from their previous application!

The employer immediately eliminates them from consideration.

If you are sending a form letter with your sportscasting job applications, stop it immediately.

Form letters make you forgettable and less likely to be hired. Instead, customize.

I'm reminded of the importance of customizing by the following message from an employer who hired a play-by-play broadcaster for his university.

"A friendly reminder to all job applicants: Please include something, ANYTHING, on why they would either like to work for me or for [our university]. It is staggering and disconcerting how many applications I have received which don't do that."

Customize your letters. Form letters save time but do much more harm than good. They are apparent to employers, and the lack of effort to submit a form letter is sure to leave the impression you are lazy. Instead, invest time to customize your letters and dramatically increase your chances of receiving a favorable reply.

Spend 15 minutes researching the company and the person you are contacting, then devote a sentence or two to explaining your interest in the position. Don't go overboard. Just do enough to show you didn't pick the employer randomly. Tell the employer why you want to work for THEM versus anyone else.

If your opening paragraph could work for more than one employer, it's not personal enough.

Here are suggestions for the kinds of differentiators you might cite:

- Radio or TV station ratings
- Being the flagship for a local pro team
- Low management turnover
- Low talent turnover
- Community involvement
- Creative marketing
- The reputation of ownership

You can also cite something about the community—you grew up there, have family in the area, vacationed there, or whatever. Being station-specific is most effective, but being market-specific is helpful, too.

Another cool thing is complimenting the employer about something they accomplished in their career. One TV job applicant told the station's sports director what he liked about the demo the sports director posted on his LinkedIn page.

Still not convinced of the need to customize your letters? Read the following message that was sent to me by a major market sports radio employer:

"Jon, in the interest of helping the industry grow, I wanted to send this along to you. This is a pet peeve of mine: potential hires sending blanket emails, just changing the name they address it to.

"Why would I hire or take a chance on someone who doesn't take the time to get to know what he's trying to get involved with?

"It's great that he is trying to sell himself, but he should customize it to the person he contacts. Otherwise, it looks like he's doing a cut-and-paste job. I don't need cookie-cutter hosts; I need creative thinkers who can provide more than the 'usual' pitch. And when I see someone who isn't offering anything more than a name change, it hits my trash folder pretty quickly."

Customizing your letter to the position you are applying for means you can no longer send the same one to every employer. Sorry to be the bearer of bad news, but lazy doesn't win in the sportscasting job market. Do your homework; personalize your letter.

SELL YOURSELF

You might find this fact about cover letters stunning:

Not all employers read them.

That's right. Many sports broadcasting employers rely exclusively upon demos and resumes to decide whom to interview. **You can make a great first impression on the rest of employers by writing a thoughtful cover letter.**

Here are nine keys to successfully selling yourself in your cover letter:

1. State the reason for your letter.

Make the opening sentence a statement of the job you are applying for. Don't just say you're applying for the "open position." They may have several. Complete the opening paragraph using the customization techniques covered on the previous pages.

2. Make it about the employer.

The cover letter is about what you can do for the employer, not what they can do for you. Phrases like, "I want this job because it's a great next step for me" are common mistakes.

3. List only your relevant experience.

Lead your second paragraph with a statement of your relevant experience. If a radio station is looking for a football and basketball play-by-play voice, there's no need to state that you have also called hockey. Focus on your experience that is relevant to the position.

4. Omit self-opinions.

Self-opinions mean nothing to employers. No one has ever written in a cover letter they are a slacker who doesn't get along with co-workers. Employers *will* listen to opinions that others have of you, but they couldn't care less about what you think of yourself. Instead, sell yourself with facts. For example:

Opinion: I am a great writer.

Fact: I am a sports update anchor/reporter at my local radio station.

Opinion: I am hard-working.

Fact: I have four years of experience in minor-league baseball media relations and play-by-play.

Opinion: I get along well with my co-workers

Fact: My experience includes anchoring, reporting, and shooting videos.

Also under the umbrella of self-opinions is, "I feel as though I would be a quality candidate for this opportunity."

Of course you do. Otherwise, you wouldn't be applying. Exclude this throwaway line.

5. Don't repeat your resume.

Your cover letter and resume are separate documents for a reason. Don't try to summarize everything you have done in your cover letter—that is the purpose of your resume. As explained above, use your letter to sell yourself and highlight your relevant experience to the position.

And don't try *too* hard to sound fabulous. There's no need for smoke and mirrors. By simply stating your experience relevant to the position, you will be ahead of 80% of applicants who aren't doing it.

Your cover letter is often the first impression an employer will have of you. Make it count.

6. Avoid hyperbole.

Don't lay it too thick when stating your interest in a position. At least 20% of cover letters I read say, "This job would be a dream come true" or "This would be my dream job." I've seen people apply for two jobs just days apart, writing in their letters that both jobs were their "dream come true." Jobs are like spouses—there are many with which you could be equally happy. Besides, is calling high school baseball your dream job over being the voice of the Yankees?

Saying, "It would be an honor" to work for the employer sounds similarly disingenuous. You are applying for a sportscasting job, not a position of royalty.

Phrases like "dream job" and "it would be an honor" are also cliché. Be different. Be better.

7. State your intent to follow up.

In your closing paragraph, tell the employer when you will follow up. Few people win in the job market without polite persistence; following up is the first step towards that.

Also, in the closing paragraph, add the name, title, and phone number of a reference who can provide additional information about your qualifications.

8. Show your personality.

Sportscasting is an entertainment industry, so show personality when introducing yourself to an employer. One sportscaster started a cover letter asking, "Has WALB ever employed a middle school long jump champ? Well, I would be excited to present you with that opportunity!" She closed her letter, stating, "By the way, I know you're on the edge of your seat—my long jump record was 15'6"."

9. Be brief.

If you step onto an elevator with an employer, you have 10 seconds to tell them why they should hire you. It's called an elevator pitch. Use your elevator pitch in your cover letter. Keep it to two-thirds of a page, max. The longer your letter, the less time most employers will give it.

Writing a 60-second radio commercial is easier than writing a 30, but the 30 is usually more effective. Similarly, shorter cover letters are more challenging to write but often pack a bigger punch.

Returning to our elevator analogy, imagine you enter one with the hiring manager for a position you want. Will you mumble a quick hello while staring at your shoes? Or will you confidently extend your hand, look them in the eyes, smile warmly, and spend your 10 seconds together stating the most relevant reasons they should hire you? You accomplish the latter when you thoughtfully sell yourself with a well-written cover letter.

BE PROACTIVE

The most iconic shot of Michael Jordan's career was in Game 6 of the 1998 Finals against Utah. It was his buzzer-beater over Bryon Russell to secure Jordan's sixth title with Chicago. MJ didn't pass to Dennis Rodman or anyone else on the floor at that moment. Jordan wanted to control his fate. He knew Chicago's best chance to win was if he was in control. Closing cover letters is like MJ closing games: you want to maintain control as long as possible.

Keep the ball in your hands by giving the employer a date upon which you will follow up to introduce yourself briefly. Add that you'll leave a message if you get their voicemail.

Too many people make the mistake of saying, "Thank you for reviewing my stuff. I hope to hear from you." It doesn't further your application. Waiting to hear from the employer is the equivalent of MJ giving up the ball with a championship on the line.

Keep the ball in your hands.

WHAT NOT TO DO: REAL COVER LETTER DISASTERS

It's fun when employers share crummy cover letters with me.

Here are two examples of dumb things sportscasting job applicants have written in cover letters—and why you want to avoid making similar mistakes.

1. Smarter-Than-Thou Syndrome

"I've performed every duty in the job summary and fulfill the knowledge, skills, and abilities you are looking for. I'm also not too shabby of an editor. Not to be snotty, but I could point out the spelling errors in the job summary if you'd like."

"Not to be snotty." That's nothing more than a warning that you're about to spew something snotty. Don't criticize the job description.

Regardless of who wrote it, you're criticizing the employer you want to work with.

2. Better-Than-Thou Statements

"I'm better than what you currently have in Afternoon Drive."

While that may be true, the program director you're trying to impress may be the one who hired that host. By criticizing the host, you are attacking the person you are asking for a job. Don't do that.

Read your cover letter as if you are the hiring manager. If you're offended, fix it.

This book's appendix contains a cover letter rubric. It will let you know if your letters are helping or hurting your job market efforts.

PRESENTATION

PRESENT YOURSELF WITH DRIP

I'll never forget the guy in the suit.

There were eight students in a college class I visited. Most dressed like typical college students. T-shirts, backward baseball caps, and oversized jeans were the rule. One young guy, though, wore a suit and tie. He set himself apart so much that I still remember his name. Aiden.

Aiden had drip; he had style.

Presentation counts. Applying Aiden's approach in the job market will help you stand out.

Here are seven simple steps to present yourself as a cut above:

1. Have a website.

Employers conduct today's job market online. Having a website helps ensure the first thing employers find when searching your name is something you want them to see.

You are a sportscasting brand. If a brand doesn't have a website, it doesn't exist. A website also allows you to share your demos and resume with employers simply by sending the link to your home page.

2. Avoid attachments.

Sending demos and resumes to employers as email attachments is like driving your car with the parking brake on. You might still get where you want to go, but it will take longer and be more difficult.

Write your cover letter in your email. Everything else employers need from you should be on your website.

Someone applying to be the voice of a college sports program might send five attachments: a cover letter, resume, and one file each for football, basketball, and baseball play-by-play. On top of that, the files likely don't include the applicant's name because that's generally not something we do when titling files on our computer. Imagine, though, that you are the employer. You've received 100 applications, each with five attachments you had to download and retitle with each applicant's name.

It's a time-consuming headache.

Let your application be an island amid stormy waters, one that gives the employer a respite from hassle.

Another reason to avoid attachments is an employer's inbox will fill quickly with large audio and video files. If you aren't among the first to apply, your application might not reach the inbox.

Finally, attachments are one way bad guys try to gain access to people's computers. If the tech department at an employer's office hasn't reset email filters to accept a bunch of emails with attachments from job applicants, your email might not make it through the filter.

Think of attachments as job market poison. Avoid them. Make it easy to hire you.

3. Write your cover letter in the email.

Cover letters are another thing job seekers often send as attachments. Instead, write your cover letter IN your email to an employer.

4. Close the YouTube door.

If you host demo reels on YouTube, embed the videos on your website instead of sending employers the URL to a YouTube page. The latter is a less-than-professional presentation of yourself. Plus, there are a lot of visual distractions on a YouTube page. If an employer clicks one of the videos YouTube suggests they might also like, they may never return to what you want them to see. There are examples of job applicants sending employers to YouTube, then the employer hiring a different candidate who they found in YouTube's recommendations of similar videos.

5. Upload one document.

When applying for a job through an employer's website, upload your cover letter and resume as a single document. Surprisingly, corporate websites often don't provide a place to upload your demo. Therefore, include the link to your website in the document header to ensure employers can access your demo. And make the document you upload a PDF to ensure an employer can open it. Don't submit a resume created in an app that an employer might not have.

6. Be uniform.

Use the same letterhead on your cover letter and resume. Uniformity looks professional.

7. Apply to the hiring manager.

After completing an online application, also apply directly to the likely decision maker—TV news directors, radio program directors, and general managers for minor league sports. In your cover letter, clarify that you have already applied online as requested in the position description, but state that you also want to introduce yourself personally.

Doing these things will help you stand out like a lion in a room full of house cats. Be the Aiden, the guy in the suit.

FOLLOW UP

STAND OUT INSTEAD OF STANDING STILL

A sportscaster called to vent about the job market: he's worked in small and mid-markets for over a decade but has struggled to earn more significant opportunities. I asked what he was doing to follow up his applications.

His answer was stunning.

He said he doesn't follow up.

"My ability should speak for itself. I don't feel I should have to brown nose anyone for the sake of getting a job," the sportscaster stated.

My jaw nearly cracked when it hit the floor.

Another sportscaster said, "I used to just send resumes out into the void and hope they'd speak for themselves. When I first started, I didn't follow up. When I found out I needed to, it was still a struggle because I'm nervous on the phone." Understandable, but not acceptable.

It's called the job market for a reason. You have to market yourself. The top 15% of applicants are equally talented. What are you going to do to set yourself apart within that group?

The Savannah Bananas set themselves apart in baseball by doing things differently. Things like unlimited concessions and dancing base coaches make the Bananas memorable. Even owner Jesse Cole stands out by wearing a yellow tuxedo every day.

You can stand out in the sportscasting job market by applying Cole's motto when following up on your applications: **"Stop standing still and start standing out."**

Do's and Don'ts for Following Up

A TV sports anchor/reporter applied for a job. He hadn't heard from the employer for two weeks, so he followed up with an email. He explained that he applied, in part, because he and his family regularly vacationed in the TV station's city.

Shortly thereafter, he finally heard from the employer. They set up an interview, and he got the job.

He won by following up.

"I rarely used to follow up," he says. "When I did, I was doing what everyone else was doing by saying things like, 'I'm just checking to see if you got my stuff.' Now I make sure that my [follow-ups] are highly personalized."

Garrett Jones prioritized following up when he applied for a position on Boise State University's play-by-play team. He recalls, "The process was three rounds long. I made sure to send a polite note after each round. Nothing crazy. For example, after Round Two, I watched one of the school's volleyball matches and sent a note complimenting the production quality."

Jones got the job.

Keep your name in front of the employer at least once a week after your introductory phone call.

The following do's and don'ts will help you create a strategy for following up on your sports broadcasting job applications.

DO these things to follow up:

1. First use the phone.

Calling demonstrates the confidence and aggressiveness sportscasting employers covet. It also allows employers to hear your personality. A sportscaster who accepted a job in minor league baseball says the hiring manager told him his follow-up call put him on the employer's radar as "someone worth interviewing."

Another sportscaster called a junior hockey team owner to follow up on an application. He serendipitously caught the owner while the owner was driving. The owner gave him an impromptu interview and hired him several days later.

2. State why and what.

State two things in your follow-up call, whether you get the employer or their voicemail: 1) Why you want to work for them. Research them, then state one or two things that appeal to you about their station or community. 2) Your relevant experience. What is on your resume that is a good fit for this position?

Remember what Garrett Jones said, "I just want to be sure you received my stuff" is a standard but weak follow-up. The chances are overwhelmingly likely they did. Asking about the hiring timeline is another common but bad idea. Generic follow-ups like those do nothing to further your application.

3. Don't call again.

Only your initial follow-up should be via telephone. Calls are obtrusive because they can be inconvenient and take more of the employer's time. Subsequent follow-ups should be via email, snail mail, smoke signal, or carrier pigeon—anything but by telephone.

A hockey broadcaster says, "I've found to avoid getting lost in the shuffle, sending short but personal follow-up emails helps get responses one way or the other."

4. Occasionally ignore "no calls please."

A former Chicago sports radio program director said when he was job-seeking, he always called when an ad said, "No calls, please." It made him stand out because nobody else was doing it. Personal contact with an employer gives you an edge.

Some employers will immediately discount you for calling. They'll wonder how coachable you'll be if you don't follow instructions in your application.

Other employers write "no calls please," yet appreciate when job seekers follow up via phone because it shows a degree of determination they respect.

Weigh each situation individually. If you know someone who knows the employer, ask the person how they think the employer would feel about you calling.

Definitely don't phone if the no-call request is in ALL CAPS, especially if preceded by the word absolutely or followed by an exclamation point.

5. Be politely persistent.

If an employer is not going to hire you, make them tell you no. Being creative is a great way to be politely persistent. More on that momentarily.

6. Stop at five.

If you've made five contacts with an employer and all have gone unreturned, stop. They aren't interested.

DON'T make these mistakes...

1. Ask for a reply.

Employers are especially busy. Many get annoyed when applicants ask the employer to call them. They'll call you if they're interested.

2. Ask for a critique.

You are asking employers for jobs, not critiques. Asking for a critique speaks of inexperience and a lack of respect for the employer's time.

If the employer doesn't know you and doesn't want to hire you, they probably don't want to critique you either.

Following up can be as awkward as asking someone for a date for the first time. Like dating, though, following up gets easier the more you do it. And it could lead to the next step in your sportscasting career.

Be politely persistent

Minor league baseball teams receive up to 200 applications for Director of Broadcasting/Media Relations positions. Setting yourself apart from such a large crowd might seem impossible. You can stand out, though, with a solid follow-up strategy.

The key is polite persistence.

Few people get jobs without following up on their applications; the squeaky wheel does get the grease. The trick is being persistent without being annoying, but where do you draw the line?

When I started STAA, I asked employers from several industries how often they would accept hearing from applicants before it became bothersome. The consensus was that touching base every three-to-four days was effective. They admitted that it could sometimes get annoying, but they appreciated the aggressiveness and demonstrated interest.

Based on my experience in hiring talent, I suggest following up once a week for immediate openings. That constitutes polite persistence.

The trick to polite persistence is creativity.

Sportscasting is an entertainment industry. Being unique or entertaining will give you an advantage in the job market. Job seekers inundate employers with applications. Give the employers a moment of pleasure and set yourself apart by presenting them with something they don't always see. It's just like being on the air—entertain your audience by giving them something they can't get anywhere else. Don't be boring.

FOLLOW UP CREATIVELY

An applicant for a major college play-by-play job followed up his application with a football. He wrote his name and phone number on it. The hiring manager and his employees would play catch with the ball several times a week during their lunch break. Soon, everyone knew the applicant's name and number! The person ended up getting the job. The football didn't get him hired, but it did make him memorable.

An applicant for another job initially didn't make the first cut. A creative follow-up, though, earned his work another look. He ended up getting hired.

You must present a demo, resume, and cover letter. How can you do so memorably? You don't have to be outrageous—just unique.

Here are some guidelines to help jump-start your creativity:

- Tailor your creativity to fit the position. If you are applying for a baseball job, do something with a bat or ball.
- Props are great attention grabbers. I have had job applicants send me clocks, books, coasters, framed pictures, and lunch. Years later, I still remember who sent me each thing.
- Research the employer. Send something unique to them. If they like golf, send a sleeve of balls with your name and number on them.

Here are 10 examples of what polite persistence can look like:

1. Record a 60-second video on your phone. Tell the employer why you want to work for them and state your relevant experience.

Smile. Laugh if appropriate. Be spontaneous. Show your personality. It doesn't have to be perfect. It's more relatable if it's not.

2. A personal note on a football, baseball, or hockey puck

3. Your resume and cover letter inside a shoe with a note, "I just want to get my foot in the door."

4. A bulleted list of fun facts about yourself.

5. A brief list of ideas you would bring to the position.

6. A short list of quotes about you from other people in the industry.

7. A mock segment of you performing the job you are seeking. For play-by-play, a 60-second highlights track featuring the team to which you are applying. For sports talk gigs, record a 6-to-8-minute mock show opening featuring the station name and your takes on the stories that fans in that market are discussing. For sports radio update anchor jobs, a 60 to 90-second update featuring stories from the market you are applying to. Listen to the station online, then format your update as they do theirs.

8. For TV anchor/reporter positions, research the market, then send a brief list of three yet-to-be-told local stories you'd like to cover if you are fortunate enough to earn the position.

9. Sports-themed greeting cards.

10. Ask a reference to call on your behalf.

There are a million and one ideas under the sun. Whether conservative or outrageous, choose follow-up strategies that fit your personality.

Again, if the employer isn't going to hire you, make them tell you no.

Be politely persistent and watch employers start paying more attention to you.

MAKE YOURSELF MEMORABLE

Many employers make the application process challenging to separate the industrious from the indolent. Again, distinguish yourself with consistent follow-up and be memorable.

The hockey broadcaster referenced earlier says, "Following up is vitally important. It's hard for an employer when the job gets initially posted, and they get inundated with new applications and emails."

Anyone *not* following up on their applications has no one to blame but themselves if their phone doesn't ring.

It's one thing to work hard in the job market. It's another thing to work smart.

Work smart to get hired.

Remember the advice of Savannah Bananas Owner Jesse Cole: Stop standing still and start standing out.

APPLYING FOR JOBS

BE AMONG THE FIRST TO APPLY

A radio station owner was hiring a sports director. The application instructions provided a two-week window in which folks could apply. On the second day, one submission blew away the employer. The employer hired that person before the application window expired.

There is an advantage to being among the first to apply for jobs.

Here are three reasons to submit your application early:

1. Early applicants are measuring sticks.

A strong application submitted early becomes the measuring stick by which subsequent applicants are evaluated. The standard has been set high, so fewer applicants make the second round. A great application that arrives early can reduce the number of competitors earning consideration.

2. It shows enthusiasm.

Many applicants assume an employer isn't interested if the employer doesn't respond within a few days. The same goes the other way, though. A person who doesn't apply until the end of the application window seems disinterested.

3. Applying late looks bad.

STAA has received applications on behalf of employers for more than four dozen NCAA Division I play-by-play jobs. Regardless of the application window—and some have been as long as six weeks—many people wait until the final two days to apply. It makes them look like uninterested procrastinators.

A primary reason people apply late is because they are unprepared. They don't have their demo and resume updated. Do you remember our friend who met an employer in a casino? You never know when an opportunity will arise. Always be ready so you can be among the first to apply.

ACT IMMEDIATELY WHEN AN OPENING EXISTS

The opening of a job with a great organization in his home state fired up a minor league baseball broadcaster. He knew it was open before it was public knowledge. He didn't know if he should wait for the team to publish a position description before applying.

Never wait!

I knew a team that had an opening immediately after their season ended. When I contacted them, they said, "We will hire that position after the Baseball Winter Meetings in December. We won't consider anyone who reaches out to us before then."

Guess what?

They hired someone before the Winter Meetings. Applicants who snoozed missed the opportunity.

Another team with an opening told me they wouldn't solicit applications. "We already have a short list," they said. People who knew the position was open did not get to throw their names into the hat because the team never solicited applications.

A third team conveyed annoyance about me wanting to know if they were accepting applications for an opening I knew they had. They also hired someone without soliciting applications.

Apply as soon as you learn of a job opening. An employer who won't accept your application because it was unsolicited is not one for whom you want to work.

The minor league baseball broadcaster mentioned a moment ago was never a candidate for the job in his home state because he waited for a position description that was never published. Conversely, a minor league baseball team didn't publish a position description when its play-by-play job opened in 2018. However, we told STAA members it was open. One of them applied and got the job.

Don't wait for the publication of a position description to apply for a job you know is open. You might miss an opportunity.

GET YOUR NEXT JOB BY BEING DIFFERENT

An aspiring sportscaster in Los Angeles saw an opening for a sports talk radio producer in Charleston, SC. He badly wanted the job as an entry into the industry. Instead of mailing or emailing his resume to the employer, he hopped on a plane and hand-delivered it. The employer was so impressed with his gumption that he got the job.

That aspiring sportscaster was Jonas Knox, who later became a national sports talk radio host.

Brainstorm ways to stand out to get your next sportscasting job. Create two columns labeled "Normal" and "Different." Write down different approaches.

Here are some ideas to get you started:

1. Cover letter

Instead of a typical cover letter, try formatting it as a press release or presenting it as a video.

2. Resume

Rather than making your potential employer look at another standard resume, format yours like a baseball card.

3. Follow-up

Instead of a follow-up phone call, make a short video explaining to the employer why you're the person for the job.

Another alternative to the follow-up call is a token of appreciation for considering your application: a mini baseball bat, a sleeve of golf balls, or even banana bread. Whatever it might be, choose something personal to you or the employer.

Different wins in the sportscasting job market. Be different to land your next job.

GO BEYOND THE APPLICATION INSTRUCTIONS

I'm a fan of national sports radio host Jim Rome.

When Rome worked in Santa Barbara early in his career, he applied to join the new sports station in San Diego. Instead of following traditional application instructions, though, he put on an all-out blitz.

Rome regularly contacted the station's general manager, the program director, a talk show host, the general sales manager, and the station's owner. He contacted them incessantly. The program director finally responded, "Jim, we'll give you a one-week try-out. If you nail it, we'll hire you. If you don't, stop bothering us because we're growing tired of you."

Rome got the job. He ended up in the Radio Hall of Fame.

The application instructions are the minimum you should do when applying for a job.

Don't ignore them, but do more than they request.

Here are some ideas.

- A San Diego FM radio DJ records a mock show daily and sends it to the program director at the station where he wants to work.
- A sports talk host customizes a daily monologue and sends it to the program director at the sports station where he wants to work.
- A play-by-play broadcaster creates a page on his website for every application he submits. Each employer sees a web page customized to them.
- Send a video resume.
- Apply via snail mail. Nobody does it anymore. If the instructions ask you to email your resume, do that. Also put it in the mail, though, so the employer has a hard copy that can't be digitally filed and forgotten.

- Send a comprehensive portfolio instead of a simple application. Help potential employers get to know you by providing various information and media.

The options are as boundless as your creativity.

Do more than the application instructions request. Stand out.

THE CLEVER LINE THAT GOT ONE GUY AN NBA JOB

Many years ago, a college basketball and minor league baseball broadcaster learned an NBA team was seeking a new radio voice. He quickly sent his demo and resume. Days later, he received this reply, "Thank you, but the application period has closed and we're already down to our finalists."

At this point, what would you do if you were the broadcaster?

Most folks would regret not hearing about the opening sooner and move on. Not this guy, though. This broadcaster had great self-confidence and motivation. He called the team's General Manager. The conversation went something like this:

Job Seeker: This is [Name]. Last week, I sent you my demo regarding your team's play-by-play position. You replied you were no longer accepting applications.

GM: Yes, that's right. The application period closed last Wednesday. We've already chosen our four finalists.

It was at this point that the job seeker delivered a classic line:

Job Seeker: If I were a 7'9 center, would you look at me?

GM: Yes, I'm always looking for the best players.

Job Seeker: Then why would you not also look for the best broadcaster?

The team's final four became the final five, and this aggressive, creative job seeker earned the gig.

The sports broadcasting job market isn't about talent alone. It's also about making yourself memorable.

ASSESS WHETHER YOU'RE TRULY READY FOR A BIG-TIME JOB

Do you have what it takes to broadcast at an elite level—a network, NFL, NBA, MLB, or NHL?

Below are some of the skills and characteristics in demand by major employers. Evaluate yourself honestly. It may be the gut check you need to reach the next level.

On Air

- Do you maintain a consistent, daily level of excellence?
- Is your unique personality evident?
- Are you interesting? Creative?
- Are you knowledgeable?
- Are you judicious in word choice?
- Are you concise?
- Are you a strong writer?
- Do you have good broadcasting instinct (knowing when to let it breathe, etc.)?

- Do you get to know the players and coaches?
- Do you check your personal baggage at the press box door?
- Do you put the needs of your audience ahead of your whims and desires?

Off Air

- Are you a team player?
- Are you a trusted public figure in your current job?
- Are you always mindful of how you represent your employer's brand?
- Do you have a reputation for reliability?
- Do you have a positive attitude?
- Are you low maintenance?
- Do you get to know the crew? The executives?
- Do you treat the entire crew, even the interns, with respect?
- Do you critique your work regularly?

If you can't answer yes to these questions, improve where necessary. You'll then have a shot to advance to the top.

Best Practices for Pursuing Big-Time Jobs

Most play-by-play broadcasters aspire to call games in the NFL, NBA, MLB, and NHL or for a major university.

Would it be helpful to know what to include on your demo, resume, and cover letter to impress potential employers?

You're about to find out.

I asked directors of broadcasting of NFL, NBA, MLB, and NHL teams and major universities what they want and don't want in applications. Their advice reinforces suggestions we've already shared.

Some had contradicting opinions. Ultimately, do what seems right for you.

Here is what the employers most commonly said they want to hear *in their words.*

DEMOS

1. Time and Score

"The MOST important things are time and score. And in football, down and distance. These are the most important habits to master above all."

2. Featuring your analyst

"I want to hear a good back and forth with the analyst. Call the play and then lay out for your analyst to do their thing."

3. Insider perspective

"Insight from practice or film that fans don't have access to. In this technology age, fans have access to just about everything online. They don't get to come to practice or sit in the film room. Make those two count in your favor by referencing them in the broadcast and providing good insight from what you saw."

4. Setting the stage

"At the beginning of the broadcast, give the fans a verbal 'visual' of the scene. Describe things like how warm/cold it is, the smell in the air, the mood on campus, etc."

5. A less scripted postgame

"Use bullet points to lead your way, but don't sound robotic and scripted."

6. Less audio

"I don't need an entire game. I also want to hear the analyst, not just the mechanics of the play-by-play guy. I want to hear more than just screaming on a touchdown. Don't just show me great highlights. I also want to hear how you work the analyst into the broadcast."

7. No music

"Don't put music under your highlights. I can't hear your highlights. This isn't a music video."

8. Variety

"The smart thing is to give me as much as you can and give me variety—highlights, an interview, and [for baseball] at least one inning of play-by-play. If you want to send a whole game, that is fine. I'll eventually listen to it if you make it far enough into the process. Not having enough on your demo can hurt you. Having too much cannot. I don't have to listen to all of it."

9. No FTP sites

"Don't post large audio files on FTP sites (file sharing sites like WeTransfer and Hightail). I received some of those, and the links had expired by the time I went to access them." (FYI—most FTP sites keep links active for just three to seven days. DropBox and Google Drive don't put expirations on links).

10. Be online

"If your demo and resume are not online, you're not keeping up with changes in the market."

RESUMES

1. Lean

"Your resume speaks for you. Anything more than a one-page resume is ridiculous. It usually works against you. That much detail means you are fibbing somewhere, or else why have you had so many jobs?"

2. Relevant

"I want to see what you've done in chronological order. I want to see your education. Non-sports stuff is unimportant. Tweak the resume to fit the job. I don't need notable achievements, awards, or press clippings. Those things are just someone's opinion. I can get online and read blogs if I want the opinions of others."

COVER LETTERS

1. Don't assume

"This is the biggest thing, and it happens almost in every case: everybody, almost to a person, in their intro letters and emails and phone calls, tells me they are the absolute right person for the job. People assume we are looking only for someone to do x number of games. We wanted somebody to be an ambassador for the team, the face of the team in the market."

2. Be you

"The cover letter is more valuable than the resume. It is the first impression. I like the English language. It says something about you. Resumes are very basic. Cover letters are like someone walking in for an interview and seeing how they are dressed. It isn't even so much content as, 'Are you personable?'"

MISCELLANEOUS

1. Curiosity

"If you call me, spend three seconds asking a question or two. For example, 'What are you and what are you not looking for?' 'Why are you looking for that?' 'What doesn't work for you?' Try to learn a little bit about what's going on."

2. Smart references

"Recommendations need to be well placed and need to be key recommendations. Be smart with email and phone call recommendations. Make it a couple of well-placed ones. Don't offer five or six recommendations from people I have never heard of."

3. Judicious reference calls

"Don't have five people call me [on your behalf]. It gets to be a bit much, especially when one is a guy with whom someone did high school football. Your talent is going to get you to the next round. It isn't about who made a call for you—not in the first round (of cuts). Recommendations can help in later rounds."

When applying for big-time jobs, it is more important to provide what employers want than to present what you want to share.

PROSPECTING WITH BIG-TIME EMPLOYERS

Prospecting for elite jobs like network TV sportscasting requires a different introduction strategy than contacting managers for typical sportscasting positions.

Follow these five critical dos and don'ts to make the most of cold contacting major employers.

DO: Send an email with a LINK to your demo.

DON'T: Include attachments on your email.

DO: Send an updated demo link every 6 to 8 months.

DON'T: Send an updated demo link whenever you add new material.

DO: Be patient. Major employers have packed schedules. Their "downtime" to listen to demos is usually June-July.

DON'T: Email to ask if they've reviewed your demo yet.

DO: Use your BEST material, uncut.

DON'T: Send only highlights.

DO: Be politely persistent by emailing every six months or so. Let the employer know if you've had any cool opportunities since you last checked in.

DON'T: Take up valuable inbox space by making contact more often than 6 months.

USE THIS SWEET TRICK TO GET IN FRONT OF EMPLOYERS

Remember my earlier story about Jonas Knox, the guy hired after flying from Los Angeles to Charleston to hand-deliver his resume?

Knox understood the advantage of letting an employer connect a person to the paper.

You have two primary options to try to meet an employer in their office:

1. Schedule a time.

Having an appointment is always better than stopping by unannounced. Here is some advice for making the request:

- Tell the employer you're in town for three days. It doesn't matter if you're not—tell them you are. It makes it harder for them to use "I'm busy" as an excuse not to see you.
- If your purpose is to follow up on an application, tell them.
- Take the indirect approach to introduce yourself for potential future opportunities. Telling the employer you want to ask about a job will turn them off. Instead, ask for their advice for your job search, request a station tour, or seek their thoughts on industry issues. Whatever you do, DON'T ask for a job.
- Request just 10 minutes. It indicates you're respectful of their time. If they like you, they'll give you more.

2. Drop by unannounced.

If you are unable to schedule an appointment, stop by unannounced. Here are two tips and two creative ideas for maximizing your chances:

- Call the station to be sure the employer is in.
- If the employer can't see you immediately, wait in the lobby. All day, if necessary. They have to come out sooner or later. They'll be incredibly impressed by your determination and

patience, or they'll think you're a creepy stalker. The potential payoff is worth the risk.

- Bring a box of donuts. It's a sweet trick. Tell the receptionist you must personally hand them to the PD. Slip your resume into the box.
- Give flowers or candy to the receptionist. They will be more eager to help you in your quest.

Employers prefer to hire people they know. Meeting someone in person is the best way for them to get to know you.

FIVE MORE WAYS TO STAND OUT IN A CROWDED INDUSTRY

The Florida Marlins once received 250 applications for their radio play-by-play position. It is still the most significant number of applicants I have heard of for a sports broadcasting position.

How do you stand out in a crowd that big?

Few things will be more frustrating in your career than repeatedly getting passed over for jobs when you are as good as the people landing the positions. How often have you told yourself, "If only someone would give me a chance?"

Talent alone isn't enough in the sports broadcasting job market. You aren't just a personality. You are a brand. **If you aren't building your brand, your career is dying.**

Your online presence is within your control.

Gail Sideman owns PUBLISIDE Personal Publicity. She teaches sportscasters (and athletes) how to market and publicize themselves —how to build their brand. She spoke about it at an STAA seminar.

Here are five suggestions from Gail to set yourself apart online:

1. Improve your social media game.

Remember that nothing you post on social media is ever truly gone. Know that some things you share won't sit well with your bosses. Remember what your mom used to say, "If you don't have something nice to say, don't say it at all."

2. Share some smart stuff.

There's a whole world that exists outside of sports. Prove you know it by sharing links to information or thoughts about great books you read. Reading will also add depth and context to your sports broadcasts.

3. Scrub your social media.

Read past social media posts and delete ones with pictures of you partying or posts featuring colorful language. Partying hard makes you look irresponsible, and too many expletives can damage your credibility as a sports news source.

4. Resist lashing out.

Keep your social media posts positive and encouraging. It's cliché, but haters hate. Ignore those people. Don't ever get into petty online fights with social media followers.

5. Start a podcast.

Podcasting is a great way to increase your relevance and profile and to start new professional relationships.

Sportscasting in the 21st century goes past just being on-air. Employers expect you to use social media to promote upcoming broadcasts and stay engaged with your audience.

Social media is also an essential part of building your brand. Use it wisely.

TIPS FOR FINDING EMPLOYER EMAIL ADDRESSES

The giveaway that a play-by-play broadcaster is ill-prepared is when they consistently hesitate to identify players. In the job market, the giveaway that someone is insufficiently motivated is complaining they can't find an employer's contact information.

How do you find email addresses for sports broadcasting employers? Refuse to be denied.

Here are five strategies that will usually get the address you want:

1. Websites

Start simple. Look on the employer's website. You might have to dig a little, but the email address you seek is often there. It's surprising how many people fail to make this minimal effort.

2. Google it

The answer to everything is on the Internet.

3. Get close

If the employer's email isn't on the company website, find the address for someone else within the organization. The structure of email addresses within a company is usually uniform. Ex: first initial last name@workplace.com.

4. Guess, then Google

If you can find the suffix for the company's e-mail address—for example, @staatalent.com—there are only a handful of first initial, first name, last initial, and last name combinations for the prefix. Google the various combinations; you'll often find which one it is.

5. Call the office

If you can't find the address, call the office. Ask whoever answers the phone for the email address you seek. Don't tell them you're a job seeker, though. Instead, state you're so-and-so from whatever your current media affiliation is. That gives you credibility. Or tell them you sent an email to what you thought was the proper address but that it bounced back to you, so you're calling to get the correct address.

Everyone has an email address. You'll usually find what you're looking for with some digging.

Again, refuse to be denied.

What to do when you don't meet minimum requirements

Your perfect next job just opened. The responsibilities fit your strengths, it's at a station for which you want to work, and in a market where you want to live. The catch is you don't meet the minimum experience outlined in the position description.

Do you apply anyway?

Yes.

Employers publish minimum requirements so less talented broadcasters will eliminate themselves. Less confident sportscasters will see minimum experience requirements and think, "I already believe I'm not good enough yet. The three-to-five-year minimum requirement convinces me not to apply."

Radio and TV employers are no different than NBA general managers. They care less about your experience than about how good you are. The NBA drafted Kobe Bryant and Kevin Garnett from high school even though they lacked the college experience teams generally prefer.

If you believe you can handle the job and can say without bias that you are good enough to work for that employer in that market, apply.

An exception is major college and major pro sports play-by-play. You must be good enough *and* have a resume that the university or team can sell to its fans.

Recent college grads often wonder if experience gained on campus radio and TV stations counts toward minimum experience requirements. It does for entry-level jobs. Otherwise, if a position description states three to five years of experience is required, they mean in commercial broadcasting. Still, if you have just two years in commercial broadcasting but know you are ready for the next step, apply anyway.

Employers generally want the best people, regardless of experience.

KNOW HOW MUCH OF YOUR TV REEL EMPLOYERS ACTUALLY WATCH

Wouldn't it be awesome to know if an employer watched your TV reel and for how long they watched it?

You will know these things if you host your reel on YouTube.

YouTube analytics provides two key pieces of info about your TV reel:

1. Who is watching.

YouTube analytics reveals the states and times when viewers watched your reel. If you applied last week for a job in Dallas and see that someone in Texas watched your reel on Thursday, you can feel confident it was the employer to whom you applied.

2. How much of your reel people are watching.

This one is huge. YouTube analytics tells you the average time people watch your reel. Knowing where people stop watching your video allows you to replace the boring parts with better content.

These two YouTube tips will help boost your confidence and enhance your chance for success in the TV sportscasting job market.

A SIX-STEP PLAN TO HIDE YOUR JOB SEARCH FROM YOUR EMPLOYER

A sports talk host had been at his station for many years. When a better time slot opened at a cross-town station, he mentioned to his producer and board op that he had applied. His boss soon heard the news. Within hours, he fired the host.

Looking for your next job while currently employed is not uncommon. The best time to look for a job is when you already have one. However, there are innovative ways to do it.

Here are six dos and don'ts when applying for work with another employer:

1. Don't tell your boss.

Many employers believe, "If you don't want to be here, we don't want you here." **With few exceptions, the only good time to tell your boss you're looking is when you've accepted an offer.**

2. Don't apply within the same company without permission.

Chances are strong that the boss you want to work for will contact your current employer if they work for the same ownership. Again, "If you don't want to be here..."

3. Don't tell coworkers you're looking.

The more people who know you're searching, the more likely somebody will reveal your secret.

4. Don't use your work email for employment pursuits.

Your boss has the right to read email correspondence within your work account. I know a sportscaster who lost his job for this reason.

5. Do seek advice.

If you must miss work for an interview but fear telling your boss, ask your prospective new boss how they would handle it. Perhaps you can Zoom or plan your visit on your day off. If you must miss work, use a sick day or cite personal reasons.

6. Don't post evidence of your trip on social media.

You'd hate for your boss to bust you like Ferris Bueller at the Cubs game. I know a dude in San Diego who called in sick to attend a weekday afternoon Padres game. The next day, the newspaper's front page featured a story about the unseasonably warm weather. The guy was among the Padres fans in the accompanying picture. Busted!

And here's a fun Rule No. 7: "Don't mail applications from a post office where your boss's wife works." A talented anchor wanted out of Amarillo. He was at the post office weekly, mailing demos to various stations. He didn't realize his boss's wife worked there. She saw him regularly. When it came time to renegotiate his contract, one point he tried to stress to management was the tremendous loyalty he had to the station. His boss replied, "I don't even want to hear that BS. My wife tells me you're at the post office every week mailing off tapes to try to get the hell out of here."

Be aggressive in your job search. But be smart.

FIND UNPUBLISHED OPENINGS

ACCESS UNADVERTISED JOB OPPORTUNITIES

One way to find and even anticipate job openings is to be a forensic sportscasting industry analyst.

In-N-Out is a popular California-based hamburger chain. Fanatic customers like to brag about their knowledge of In-N-Out's "secret menu." The menu is a way to customize the restaurant's burger, fries, and milkshake options. And it's not a secret—anyone can use it if they spend time to learn it.

There is a "secret menu" of sportscasting jobs. It is available to anyone who spends the time to learn it.

Here are seven tips for accessing the "secret menu" of sportscasting jobs:

1. Watch the headlines.

Pay attention to industry headlines. When you see a broadcaster leaving, contact their former employer immediately to express your interest. Don't wait for a position description to be published. Contacting the employer before they post the job publicly ensures you'll beat the rush.

2. Watch management turnover.

A new radio program director or TV news director usually takes roughly two months to evaluate their inherited talent. Changes often follow. Reach out to new managers when it gets close to that two-month mark.

3. Contact local schools.

This is a fabulous tip for play-by-play broadcasters. Ask local schools if they need someone to help with their streaming broadcasts. Most schools use multiple freelancers for ESPN+ and other streaming broadcasts.

4. Contact local Internet broadcasters.

Let local streaming companies know your desire to help cover high school or small college games.

5. Attend industry events.

Meeting employers in person is the most significant advantage a job seeker can have. Conferences and seminars are ideal for this. The National Sports Media Association's annual awards weekend in North Carolina is a gold mine. Most state broadcaster associations also hold annual events.

6. Be a source of information.

Send links to articles or anything else you think might be helpful to a potential employer. Begin establishing yourself as a "here's something for you" person instead of a "what do you have for me?" person.

7. Use LinkedIn.

Sports broadcasting employers use LinkedIn to meet job seekers. Use the platform to introduce yourself.

When you apply for jobs everyone knows about, you might be among 100 applicants. When you access the sportscasting job market's "secret menu," your chances for employment are considerably greater.

Prompt others to recommend opportunities

I love reading books. One of my all-time favorites is *When Pride Still Mattered* by David Maraniss. It's a fabulously researched biography about legendary Green Bay Packers coach Vince Lombardi. Another great read is *Phog*, a biography about storied University of Kansas basketball coach Phog Allen. And I'm a Kansas State Wildcat saying that!

I didn't discover these books on my own. People recommended them to me.

You can find many job openings at websites like staatalent.com. However, like the books people tell me about, **the best sportscasting opportunities will often be unpublicized openings someone recommends.**

Here are two strategies to prompt people to recommend job opportunities to you:

1. Tell everyone you're looking.

People won't help if they don't know you need it. When you tell people you're looking for a job, they can share opportunities that will be a good fit. Exercise discretion, though, about who you contact if you don't want your current employer to know you are looking.

2. Use the referral request.

I love Kansas State football. I graduated from K-State and was a walk-on in the basketball program. However, it's the football program that I've long had a passion for because of its legendary coach, Bill Snyder.

Coach Snyder's teams entered and exited the stadium as a group. It was a show of solidarity and strength in numbers. You can apply the "strength in numbers approach" to your job market pursuits by using the referral request.

The idea is to talk to people—not with the expectation that they will hire you, but that they might refer you to someone who will.

The referral request prompts people you know to help you in the job market. It is the most successful strategy for finding unadvertised sportscasting opportunities. It is also a great way to build relationships that will benefit you throughout your career.

There are two simple steps to the referral request:

1. Contact someone you know.

Ask an acquaintance if you can schedule a brief conversation about how to conduct a successful job search. You're not asking for a job so don't include a resume with your request. At the end of the conversation, ask if they will refer you to two or three other people with whom you can have a similar discussion.

If you struggle to start the referral request because you're unsure how to ask, sample emails are provided at the end of this chapter.

2. Contact your new referrals.

When you contact the people somebody referred you to, say, "I'm in the job market. Our mutual friend Joe Smith suggested I contact you. Joe thought you would have some great advice." Again, if you approach via email, do not include a demo or resume with your letter.

At the end of your call, ask who else they recommend you call for a similar conversation. When you contact those folks, you can say so-and-so referred you. By your third call, someone usually will tell you where there is an unadvertised opening.

In addition to finding job leads, you are building a strong network of professional relationships.

These people are likely to help because you come referred by someone they know; they want to do a favor for that person. Plus, you're asking for advice versus a job, and you're flattering this person by saying you believe their wisdom can benefit you.

Here are templates for the two steps in the referral request sequence:

Email #1: The one you send to someone you know.

Dear Joe,

I'm looking for my next sports broadcasting opportunity. With your experience in the industry, I'm sure you would have some great advice to share.

May we schedule a brief 10-minute call so I can ask for your suggestions?

Jon

Email #2: The one you send to a person you've been referred to.

Dear Mike,

Our mutual friend Joe Smith suggested I contact you for advice.

I'm looking for my next sports broadcasting opportunity. Joe said you might have some wisdom that will be helpful to me.

Can we please schedule a brief 10-minute call so I can ask you some questions? I know you are busy, so I will understand if it doesn't fit your schedule.

Please let me know.

Thank you, Mike.

Regards,

Jon Chelesnik

USE COLD CONTACTING EFFECTIVELY

Upon graduating from the University of Notre Dame, Mike Monaco set about cold contacting area schools with hopes of finding a college basketball job. It paid off. He earned the opportunity to call Western Michigan University men's and women's hoops on ESPN3.

The challenge of the sportscasting job market is many people are applying for relatively few publicized positions. Wouldn't it be awesome if the number of people you were trying to stand out from was closer to 10 for a given job instead of 110?

It can be.

Cold contacting is introducing yourself to employers to express your interest in unadvertised or future opportunities. It's also called prospecting and proactive outreach.

Many job opportunities are never advertised publicly—anecdotal evidence suggests up to 80%. You give yourself a greater chance to advance your career if you tap into that gold mine of opportunities. You are putting your name on the employer's radar when other job seekers aren't also vying for attention. Cold contacting works equally well for full-time and freelance opportunities.

Cold contact is a primarily ignored strategy because many people fear it. They've heard employers don't like to be cold-contacted. Not true. Employers don't like *annoying* cold contacts. However, they love meeting ambitious, talented people who present themselves professionally and creatively. An employer will be grateful to hear from you if you demonstrate you can help them.

Before getting into how to best cold contact employers, let's look deeper at the three excuses why job seekers don't do it. I initially called the excuses "reasons." I changed it, though, because calling them reasons validates them. Oxford Languages defines excuse as "an explanation put forward to defend or justify a fault." In other words, an excuse is an attempt to rationalize not doing something you should be doing.

Here are three excuses why job seekers don't cold contact:

1. There isn't an immediate opening.

We live in a society of instant gratification. Job seekers don't want to invest time in pursuing openings that don't yet exist. They need employment today, not three months from now. They don't understand that applying only for the same advertised jobs as 100 other applicants usually results in the job market taking more than three months.

2. It's awkward.

Contacting an employer for whom you want to work can be uncomfortable. Contacting one who doesn't even have a current opening can be even more unsettling. Whether you are reaching out to a radio station program director, a TV news director, or the general manager of a team, corresponding with someone who could hold the key to the next step of your career is a nerve-racking experience if you don't know what to say.

3. Fear of being a bother.

I often hear this, especially from job seekers in their 20s: "I don't want to cold contact an employer because I'm afraid of being a bother." You are only a bother if you are unprepared and your approach isn't well thought out.

The great news is these three excuses work in your favor. Because cold contacting is hard, most of your competition isn't doing it. Because it is hard, it is an easy way to set yourself apart.

The loser says, "It's too hard. I can't do it." The winner says, "It's hard, but I will find a way."

The key to successful cold contact is to target wisely. Be smart about the employers you contact. It's one thing to work hard in the job market. It's another to work smart. Build a target list using these four guidelines:

1. Less is more

Sportscasters often tell me how many demos and resumes they've sent to employers—50, 60, sometimes as many as 100. Their effort is commendable, but their efficiency leaves much to be desired. Here's why. As mentioned earlier in this book, following up your applications with polite persistence is a key to success in the job market. It is challenging to follow up 50 applications effectively.

Your job search will be more efficient and effective if you target 15 or 20 employers and follow up diligently rather than contacting 50 or 60 with little or no follow up.

2. Specificity

A common cold contacting mistake is saying, "I am interested in any opportunities at your station." That will never work. Someone who will accept any job is likely qualified for none. It also sounds desperate. Instead, know exactly the role you want to fill. And be sure it is one for which you have sufficient experience. Don't say you want to be an anchor/reporter even though your only broadcasting experience is doing play-by-play.

3. Market size

The ability to realistically assess your broadcasting ability is invaluable when cold contacting. A recent college grad who wants to work in New York, LA, or Chicago isn't going to break into those markets as a sports talk host. Getting in as a board op or a producer is a more reasonable goal. Someone with three years of experience in Sheboygan is also unlikely to get a sports talk gig in a Top 20 market, but it is reasonable they can get a gig as a sports update anchor or reporter.

Be realistic when evaluating what you are ready for in the next step of your career.

4. Geography

The places you target should be geographically desirable to you, but your chances for employment will be better if you are geographically desirable to the employer. Most employers prefer to hire regionally. They want someone who knows the local teams and their history. Hiring regionally also reduces potential relocation expenses for the employer.

Of course, choose targets in parts of the country where you would like to live. You may have family in the region, enjoy the weather, or want to try something new.

Introduce Yourself with Purpose

As we said, introducing yourself to a prospective employer can be awkward and intimidating. Remember, though, someone who presents themselves confidently and professionally is impressive. Most employers want to know more about someone like that.

Email vs. Phone

Are you hesitant to introduce yourself because the thought of the phone call makes you nervous? You're in luck. A phone call does demonstrate desirable aggressiveness and confidence and allows an employer to hear your personality.

However, email is better for two reasons:

1. Email is unobtrusive.

An employer can read it at their convenience. You don't have to worry about catching them at a bad time or in a bad mood. You want to elicit intrigue versus annoyance.

2. You can carefully choose your words for maximum impact.

A job-prospecting email is nearly identical to a cover letter message (see the chapter on cover letters in Chapter 2: Job Market). The only change is instead of stating that you are applying for a job you know is open, you state your interest in potential opportunities.

As with a job application, follow up on your cold contact. When a station has a current opening, keep your name in front of them weekly. When you are prospecting, though, weekly correspondence is too much. Every four to six weeks will ensure you don't become annoying.

Recall what we said in the section about the referral request: Asking for advice instead of employment is comfortable for the employer because they don't have to tell you no. If you ask for a job, you'll get advice. If you ask for advice, you'll sometimes get a job. Also, you'll sometimes get more attention from an employer if you ask for advice. It's flattering that you value their wisdom.

JOB INTERVIEWS

FAILURE TO PREPARE IS PREPARING TO FAIL

The best advice I share is often straight from sports broadcasting employers. In this case, it is about the telephone job interview.

The number one way to blow a phone interview is to be unprepared.

The following comments are from a minor league baseball executive who was frustrated by the experience of filling a broadcasting position.

"I'm doing a bunch of phone interviews today for the broadcast position here. I just hit a string of 3-4 guys who, when I asked 'why you?' for this job, the first thing they said was 'I really love baseball.' After a while, it takes great restraint not to respond, 'Oh, that's good because, as luck would have it, we are a baseball team!'

"I'm trying to give everyone their due, respond to all applicants, and really connect with each person on the phone. [It's frustrating] dealing with people who don't seem prepared for this call even after I told them exactly when I'd be calling. These aren't out-of-the-blue calls. I emailed everyone with dates and times I'd be calling them after asking when they were free. Part of me wants to pause the phone call and coach them up on how to handle an interview."

Fortunately, preparing for a job interview is easy. It just takes time.

When I was a kid, I received a magazine called *Highlights*. Your parents or grandparents might remember seeing it in the waiting room at a pediatrician's office when they were kids.

Highlights had a feature titled Goofus and Gallant. Goofus always did stuff the wrong way; Gallant did it the right way. The following "Yes, This Really Happened" story concerns Goofus and Gallant in the sports broadcasting job market. The examples come from a broadcasting executive.

This exec interviewed two people for a position. He interviewed Goofus first. Goofus hadn't researched the executive's background. When Goofus made a snide remark about a particular university, he was stunned when the employer replied the university was his alma mater.

When the same person interviewed Gallant, Gallant had researched so thoroughly that he not only knew where the executive attended college, but he knew the exec had been an athlete at the school.

Gallant got the job offer.

Failure to prepare is preparing to fail.

It seems too easy an answer or too simple a solution. It's not.

Be Gallant to win the job interview. Be prepared.

FIVE THINGS TO RESEARCH ABOUT YOUR INTERVIEWER

A friend once called before a job interview to ask if I could share any background info on the employer. His call reminded me how much extra preparation can set you apart.

Here are the five questions he asked me:

1. How do you describe the employer?

2. What can you tell me about his background?

3. What are his interests?

4. What is something that his past hires for this position have had in common?

5. Why is the position open?

Doing online research about the company, the market, and the person you will speak with is smart job interview prep. Researching the employer by asking questions of people who know them will provide even more specific information to help you win the interview. Doing your homework will also allow you to organically drop information into the interview that will impress the employer.

TIPS FOR WINNING THE INTERVIEW

A radio station employer in Michigan was looking for a sports director. Following a phone interview with a candidate from South Dakota, the employer thought he might have found his guy. He brought him to Michigan to meet over dinner.

That's when things fell apart.

The individual's table manners were so raw that the employer knew there was no way he could hire this person to represent his station.

Besides using your napkin if a prospective employer takes you to dinner, there are several other tips, tricks, and strategies for winning your next job interview:

1. Know there are no wrong answers.

The most important thing to understand is that most employers evaluate the interview's success on how well they get to know you. Answer truthfully and from your heart.

2. Don't try to force your answers to fit the job.

If you are interviewing for the Yankees play-by-play job and they ask you about your passion in life, you don't have to say, "Sports broadcasting and play-by-play." Doing so might sound disingenuous and like you are trying too hard.

3. Don't talk too much.

Many candidates talk themselves out of the job. Answer questions politely and thoroughly, but stay on topic and don't repeat yourself.

4. Write thank you notes.

Send a brief hand written note to each person who participated in your interview. Thank them for their time. It won't get you the job, but it can confirm that you are the right choice.

5. Stay calm, be prepared.

Your degree of nerves will be in direct, inverse proportion to your preparation.

Remember that if it's a phone interview, you don't have to maintain eye contact and can more easily take notes. You might also choose to sit in a room where you feel especially comfortable.

6. Consider taking notes.

It is perfectly acceptable to take notes during an in-person interview. It can even demonstrate an exceptional degree of interest.

7. Take a breath.

If you get nervous, pause to take a deep breath while the employer speaks or before you answer the question.

When interviewed, give honest answers that help the employer get to know you.

Appeal to the Employer's Ego

A sportscaster was a finalist for a play-by-play job at a university. The interview process included meetings with the athletic director, assistant AD, marketing staff, and coaches of the various sports the person would cover.

This individual was nailing the interviews—making a great impression in each of them. He felt good about his chances of getting the job when an administrator told him there was one last coach to meet. The candidate was warned, "This one will be tough to impress."

They escorted him down a hallway to the coach's office; he felt like a coach with a 30-second timeout to draw up a game-winning play. His mind worked furiously to develop a plan.

What he devised worked brilliantly.

Here is his three-point plan that nailed the job interview:

1. Let them brag.

The man recalled several of the coach's notable achievements, which he had read about while preparing for the interview. He asked the coach how he had gone about accomplishing such impressive feats. The coach immediately opened up, eager to brag about what he achieved. He was like a peacock showing off its beautiful tail feathers.

People love to feel important. In a job interview, **give the interviewer a chance to brag about themselves.**

2. Let them talk.

Once the coach got on a roll, the man let him keep going. He knew the coach was like most everyone else. Many people love hearing themselves more than listening to you, even in a job interview. Let the interviewer speak. They will like what they hear.

3. Say their name.

The man spoke the coach's name several times throughout the meeting. It is one of the tenants of selling. People love hearing their name, so use it naturally, but not excessively. Saying it a few times helps you connect. Saying it constantly can feel forced. By repeating the coach's name, the man further ingratiated himself.

The man was offered and accepted the position. As he told me the story of his meeting with the coach, I realized his three tips for nailing the job interview roughly paralleled the wisdom in Dale Carnegie's classic book, *How to Win Friends & Influence People*.

Consider reading Carnegie's book if you are preparing for a job interview or want to position yourself best to take the next step in your career. Another great—and free—interview prep resource is *How to Make Them Love You and Pay You Too*, also by Dale Carnegie.

QUESTIONS TO EXPECT

The more interviews you do, the more you will realize many employers ask variations of the same handful of questions. Knowing what might be coming allows you to prepare.

Here are suggestions for how to reply to common job interview questions:

1. Why are you the person for this job?

Focus your answer on relevant career experience.

2. What are your strengths and weaknesses?

Strengths are easy. For weaknesses, choose something you can spin into a positive. Or share something that used to be a weakness, then explain how you turned it into a strength. Ex: "I have difficulty saying no when people ask me for help. I need to be sure doing so doesn't come at the expense of executing my job responsibilities." Or, "I sometimes clutter my broadcasts with information because

I'm eager to show my preparation. Recently, I've been more strategic about when to use facts and stats."

3. Who do you respect and admire in the business?

Your answer helps an employer learn what they might expect from you.

4. What is your greatest accomplishment?

It doesn't have to be in sports broadcasting. An answer unrelated to broadcasting shows depth and helps an employer get to know you.

5. What ideas did you bring to your current/last job for something they hadn't been doing before?

Employers love employees who are creative and eagerly work beyond their position description.

6. Why should we feel comfortable hiring someone from out of state?

Convince the employer of your ability to quickly learn the local market, or the conference if you are interviewing for a play-by-play job. Employers want to know that you can quickly sound "local."

7. What is your experience with social media?

In most sportscasting job descriptions, Instagram, TikTok, X, and other social media platforms are typical. Be prepared with ideas for promoting their brand.

When someone asks you questions you don't know the answer to, you can respond, "I don't know, but I will look into/consider that and get back to you later today." Taking this approach can score points for you versus the sabotage you might cause by trying to fake your way through an answer.

Knowing the questions on a test would help a student prepare for and ace the exam. Preparing for common job interview questions can give you the same advantage.

Questions to Ask

"Do you have any questions for me?"

Invariably, most job interviews get to the point where the employer asks you that question. The worst response is:

"Nope, I think you pretty much answered everything."

That is a passive reply. Employers dislike passive. Instead, demonstrate your genuine interest in the position by confidently asking questions.

In the days before your interview, think about things you especially want to know, then start your questions with those. There are hundreds of other questions you might also ask. Here are some ideas:

- What do you enjoy about working for this company?
- What do you enjoy about living in this city?
- What are some traits you especially liked in past employees?
- What are some traits you didn't care for in former employees?
- What are some challenges of this position?

- If I am fortunate enough to get this position, what kind of support will I receive?
- If I am fortunate enough to get this opportunity and I do well, what are the opportunities for promotion?

There are also questions NOT to ask. Inquiring about vacation days and reserved parking places demonstrates a "what's in it for me" mentality that might cost you the job.

Be bold in asking questions. **The interview is as much about you determining if the employer is a good fit for you as vice-versa.**

SUCCEED IN VIDEO INTERVIEWS

A TV sportscaster in Georgia had a Zoom interview with an employer he desperately wanted to work with. He blew the interview because he did it in a t-shirt and gym shorts.

Another sportscaster ruined her video interview by doing it while walking down a street.

Follow these three tips for video job interviews so you don't make the same mistakes our friends did.

1. Dress appropriately.

Dress for a video job interview as you would for an in-person interview. You'll look good for the employer and feel better about yourself. We all carry ourselves with a bit more pride when dressed for success. It's like athletes say, "Look good, feel good. Feel good, play good."

2. Find a quiet spot.

Make sure you're in a quiet location. You don't want jackhammers outside, a loud television in the other room, a cackling bird (or wife. Sorry, honey), or screaming children.

3. Check your background.

Be sure whatever the employer sees in the background isn't anything you would mind them seeing or anything that would be distracting. Your dad or grandpa's circa 1976 poster of a swimsuit-clad Farrah Fawcett is probably not the best thing to have behind you when talking to a potential employer.

Treating video job interviews with the same professionalism and urgency as in-person meetings will help you avoid mistakes that can cost you the job.

How Hoosiers Helped Land a Sports Radio Job in LA

Years ago, the program director of a sports radio station in Oklahoma City applied for the same position at a Los Angeles station. Management in LA loved everything about him—his knowledge of the format, his ability to manage personalities, his proficiency working with sales and marketing departments – all of it.

There was just one thing that gave management in LA reservations about hiring him–the huge jump in market size from where he was to where they were.

When the trepidation came up in the interview, the PD replied brilliantly.

"Do you remember in the movie *Hoosiers* when the kids from Hickory walked into Hinkle Fieldhouse?" he asked the LA management team. "Their jaws were on the floor. Gene Hackman asked the players to measure the height of the hoop. It was 10 feet. He told his players that the game was the same even though the building was bigger."

That clever answer earned the man the PD job in LA.

The sports broadcasting job market isn't about talent alone. It's also about making yourself memorable. It's called the job "market" for a reason. What will you do to convince employers that you are the right person for the position?

The next time you apply for a sports broadcasting job, **anticipate the employer's hesitation about hiring you, then think about how to overcome it.** You can even proactively address it in your cover letter.

Addressing a potential concern before it becomes real might make the difference in you getting your next job.

CONTRACTS

Negotiate via email

A TV sports anchor was negotiating a new contract. He wondered if negotiating via email, phone, or in person was best. For a professional negotiator, in person is best. For the rest of us, email is the best option for two reasons:

1. Documentation

If you end up in a disagreement or in court, a written record of the conversation will be valuable. It might be imperative if you are going to have a chance to win in front of a judge.

2. Word choice

Negotiating via email provides time to construct your message carefully. You can thoughtfully consider what you want to ask for, be precise in presenting it, and choose words for maximum impact.

Email negotiation is extra helpful if you don't always think fast on your feet. The employer may come back with a response to which, at the moment, you don't have a quick or intelligent reply. You can take as much time as necessary to consider your response in an email.

KEYS FOR GETTING TO YES IN CONTRACT NEGOTIATIONS

Sportscasters are often great at one thing—sportscasting. They're often not as good at art, cooking, and automotive repair. And many aren't so good at negotiating. Shoot, if you are like I was during my sportscasting career, you're so pleased to have work you'll take whatever compensation the employer offers and not ask questions.

Some sportscasters have an agent or attorney negotiate on their behalf. It can protect the air talent from friction with their employer. Plus, non-professionals often avoid asking for what they want, fearing they'll look greedy.

If you negotiate for yourself, don't leave money on the table. You can get more value from your contract than you think.

Here are six keys for successful contract negotiations for a new or expiring contract:

1. Ask

It was either in Boy Scouts or in a fortune cookie at Double Happiness Chinese restaurant in Del Mar, CA, where I first heard, "You'll never know what you can do until you try." It applies to contract negotiations, too. All contracts have some room to negotiate, whether that means the agreement's financial and/or non-monetary aspects. The latter can often be even more valuable than salary.

2. Know the wiggle room

A large market station is more likely—and typically more able—to offer flexibility in contract terms when they want to get someone signed. Market size generally matters less, though, than the company that owns the station. Some stations try to force their standard contract on everyone; others are more willing to work to be fair.

3. Leverage

Nothing boosts your ability to negotiate a great new contract with your current employer more than leverage. Even if you have zero interest in leaving, put your work out there and see who bites. If you get crickets, negotiate smartly—but don't push so far that you put your current offer at risk. If outside interest is strong, that's your cue to negotiate boldly for the terms that really matter.

4. Persistence

Don't take an employer's first no as final. Keep selling your value. If you are negotiating with your current employer, remind them of the benefits of retaining you versus hiring someone new. Most employers hate to do the latter. They'll often find a sweetener to get a deal done.

5. Preparation

Here are three things to know and/or do when prepping for your negotiation. A) Know the reasonable value of your job based on the market. B) Know that co-workers and colleagues are almost always wrong when they tell you how much so and so makes. C) Identify the contract terms that matter most to you and prepare to compromise on less significant ones.

6. Creativity

The days when stations readily offered more money, vacation, outs, clothing allowance, etc., are essentially over. Therefore, it is critical to think creatively about other, often non-monetary ways, to improve the overall quality of a deal. An additional $5,000 annually after taxes is only worth about $125 per paycheck. Reducing a station's option to terminate without cause might be worth more in the long run (usually only an option for major market of high profile roles).

If an employer can't budge on base salary, here are four other areas where you can try to increase the value of the total compensation package:

- Paid time off for professional development.
- Cell phone allowance, especially if you are a reporter who uses a personal phone for email and/or to send video from the field.
- Bartering. Though not as common as it once was, some stations might still be willing to consider hair and or clothing trade relationships with local businesses in exchange for an on-air mention.
- Signing bonus. Some stations may have a little extra money available to give in exchange for you signing on the dotted line.

Knowing these six keys and preparing accordingly can help you get what you want in your next employment deal.

WHAT TO DO WHEN YOU ARE CONTRACTUALLY BOUND TO A BAD PLACE

A TV sportscaster was one month into a two-year contract with a new employer. Things weren't working out as he anticipated; he wanted out.

What do you do when you are contractually obligated to be someplace you don't want to be?

1. Ask out

If you are just into your contract, your employer might prefer to release you from the contract than to keep an unhappy employee around for another 23 months.

2. Buy out

It might cost you several thousand dollars, but what price do you put on your happiness?

If you can't get out, address the reason for your unhappiness. Don't like your boss? Offer to do something helpful for them that is beyond your position description. You'll both feel better about each other.

Don't like a co-worker? Learn about something that interests them, then ask them about it. You'll be surprised at how quickly taking a personal interest can turn a foe into a friend.

Don't like several co-workers? If it's more than one person you aren't getting along with, the problem might be you. Look at how you handle interoffice relationships and see what you can do differently.

Feel homesick? That feeling will be minimized once you settle into daily work and home routines. FaceTime helps a ton, too. You aren't the first person to move far from home. Nobody has died from it yet.

Don't like the weather? Weather is seasonal. It will change.

Whatever makes you unhappy at work isn't permanent. You aren't obligated to stay anywhere forever. **In the meantime, take advantage of the opportunities your employer is giving you to hone your craft and build your resume.** They are paying you to prepare yourself for your next job.

Getting paid to grow personally and professionally is a good deal.

REJECTION

SELF-EVALUATE TO MOVE FORWARD

A frustrated job seeker asked me what else he could do in the job market. I replied, "What have you already done?"

I was stunned by what I learned.

This frustrated person first told me that employers don't recognize his greatness. "It's their fault I'm not getting hired."

It's not the employer's fault.

You hire you, and you fire you. You have to make employers want to hire and keep you.

The second thing I asked this person was to show me how he addresses the five variables in the sports broadcasting job market: demo, resume, cover letter, presentation, and follow-up.

His approach was atrocious.

He thought he was doing a lot in the job market and giving great effort when he wasn't. **He wasn't paying attention to small things that add up to be big difference-makers.**

Many job seekers refuse to honestly evaluate how hard they work towards their goals—to see themselves as they are. Instead, we often blame others when things don't go our way.

Understand that sportscasting lives—yours, mine, and everyone else's—are mostly the same. We start in small markets struggling to pay our bills. As we move up, we feel underpaid, underappreciated and overworked.

Advancement rarely happens as quickly as we want it to. Teams fold. Stations change formats. Ownership changes. That stuff is not unique to you or me.

We all face the same challenges, yet some people crumble, and others thrive in the same circumstances.

Why is that?

Look at what you're doing. Honest self-evaluation is something of which we're all capable. Once you do it, you will take a big step toward your sports broadcasting goals.

USE CHANGE TO OVERCOME JOB MARKET FRUSTRATION

When an STAA member gets a job, we post their success story on our website. The stories serve as motivation to others and often provide keys for how you can win in the job market. One of my all-time favorite success stories is that of Delaney Brey.

Delaney went to work for The Media Gateway in Little Rock, Arkansas. Her story is worth mentioning because it is a typical story of job market frustration. What set Delaney apart is that, instead of stubbornly doing the same thing, she made changes.

Here is her story in her words:

"The first month after graduating, I was super discouraged when I would send in an application and hear absolutely nothing. That's when I decided to sign up for STAA. I really paid attention to the resources given for applications and follow ups. It's amazing how simple changes make all the difference. Even if it was a no, I was at least getting a response, which to me is so much better than silence."

While I appreciate Delaney touting the benefits of STAA, that isn't my purpose for sharing this. Instead, it is her observation, "It's amazing how simple changes make all the difference."
It is so true.

Small, overlooked details are application killers.

Again, there are five variables in the sportscasting job market besides talent—demo, resume, cover letter, presentation, and follow-up. If you are good enough for the jobs you are applying for but aren't hearing back from employers, look for places to revise your approach.

The definition of insanity is repeatedly doing the same thing but expecting a different result.

If your job market strategy isn't working, it is time to make changes.

An Awesome Response to Not Getting a Job Interview

A friend of mine applied for a sportscasting job for which he thought he was a perfect candidate. He had the necessary experience and ability and knew the market inside and out.

He didn't even get an interview. His response to the disappointment, though, was excellent.

He didn't gripe about bad luck, unfair treatment, or the employer not appreciating his ability. He said, "Sometimes it's difficult around here having to do every aspect of the job while working a few other places at the same time, but one day it will pay off."

How awesome is that? "One day it will pay off."

I was once at a similar place in my sportscasting career. I worked several side jobs around my primary gig at XTRA Sports 690 in San Diego to pay the bills. After five years, the payoff was getting a show on ESPN Radio Network.

In sportscasting, **the folks who get to the top aren't always the most talented. They are the ones who persevered.**

I told my friend, "Keep doing your best. Your payoff is coming."

How to Burn Bridges with Employers

Most job applicants feel qualified for the jobs for which they apply. Nearly as many are confident they will get it. On the occasions when they don't, applicants might feel emotions ranging from disappointment and frustration to disbelief. "How can this employer be so short-sighted not to see my greatness?"

Those emotions are okay. They're understandable. I have felt some of them myself in the job market. Keep them to yourself.

Expressing disappointment to employers who don't hire you burns bridges.

Here are some messages employers have shared with me from applicants who didn't get the job. We edited them for privacy:

- "Would it be possible for you to refer me to another club or position?"
- "Are there other openings within your organization that you can steer me towards?"
- "Gosh. I've been a sportswriter for my local newspaper for years. I covered an NBA team, picked the greatest players of all time for every franchise for a national magazine, and much, much more. I don't want you to think that I am displaying sour grapes; if I don't get the job I want to lose out to the best and believe me, I wish you the best with this hire. But in the future, if there is a chance to join your team, I'd like you to remember, 'That Smith can write!'"

One employer told me, "I suppose I am sort of okay with the requests for help, but that's something I would never, ever do at that moment."

Another employer said, "I received a surprising amount of pushy and despondent replies to my emails to candidates who did not get the job. I can understand applicants trying to extend communication and make something of a no, but many were over the top.

"The reactions I got after the fact would almost incline me to change my opinion of some applicants I otherwise felt fine about."

The job market is like a season for a sports team. Only one person wins at the end. Everyone else's season ends with a loss. Remembering this will make it easier for you not to take job market rejection personally.

If you feel compelled to contact the employer who didn't hire you, don't share your feelings and risk burning a bridge. Instead, congratulate them on their new hire and thank them for considering your application.

Building bridges moves you closer to the next stage of your career.

DON'T FOLLOW "NO" WITH A CRITIQUE REQUEST

A sports talk show host told me that, after he had unsuccessfully applied for a job, he asked the program director to critique his work.

I asked, "Why did you do that?"

Here are three reasons you don't want to ask hiring managers to critique your work:

1. It's not what you want from them

You want work, so don't ask for something else.

2. Employers are busy

Most employers are too busy to critique your work. They're even more unlikely to do it if they don't know you. Don't ask strangers for favors. You might get away with it if they've come to know you during the application process and there is mutual respect. Most applicants, though, don't get that far in the process.

3. It's a bad look

Asking a hiring manager to critique your work makes you look inexperienced. That's not a look that you want.

WHAT TO DO WHEN YOUR CAREER ISN'T UNFOLDING AS PLANNED

There is a veteran play-by-play broadcaster in the Midwest. We'll call him Cameron. Cameron was excited to learn three NCAA Division I football and basketball play-by-play jobs were opening. He had honed his craft, built his resume, and paid his dues.

When the time came to apply, Cameron did so with great enthusiasm, excitement, anticipation, and optimism. He followed the application instructions perfectly and followed up creatively with the employers. He felt confident he would at least get an interview.

Not making the top 20 for any of the three schools crushed Cameron. He didn't attend any of the three, lacked ties to the conferences, and didn't live near any of the schools. For these various reasons, he wasn't the right fit. He did everything right in his career but didn't even get a look.

Cameron's story is typical in the play-by-play job market.

You can do things to enhance your chances of getting a Division I play-by-play job. However, doing all the right things still doesn't guarantee you will achieve your goal.

As we get older, we sometimes realize we must change our goals. The great news is that we can still find happiness.

Instead of regretting what you don't have, be grateful for what you do have. By taking pride in always doing your best at whatever it is you are doing, you will find happiness, fulfillment, and contentment.

Five Reasons Less-Talented Sportscasters Keep Getting Jobs

We all know someone who laments that people who are less talented than them keep getting great sportscasting jobs.

Measuring ourselves against others without bias is, at the very least, challenging. For this conversation, though, let's assume a person *is* repeatedly being passed over in favor of less talented, less qualified candidates.

Here are five reasons why talented people are passed-over in the sportscasting job market:

1. Age

Younger talent costs less.

2. Bad vibes

After losing a high-profile job, one sportscaster began privately bad-mouthing his former employers to industry friends. Whether the dismissal was justified is irrelevant. Sports broadcasting is a small industry. You can quickly tarnish an excellent reputation if you complain to enough people.

3. Insincerity

Sometimes, the more talented sportscaster doesn't get the job because they aren't genuine. Be sincere in building relationships, nurture them, and give more than you take.

4. Hard to work with

Managers often pass over talented sportscasters who don't play well with others. Get along with bosses and co-workers. Treat behind-the-scenes people well. Don't be demanding. Don't be a diva. Stay humble. Be easy to work with.

5. Poor attention to detail

Reputation alone won't always open doors for you. Be sure your demo features what employers need, your resume is effectively formatted, your cover letter is well-written, you present your applications professionally, and you are intelligently following up with employers.

Talent is a reason people get hired in sportscasting, but it isn't the only one.

THE TWIN KILLERS IN THE SPORTSCASTING JOB MARKET

Attitude and anger are twin killers in the sportscasting job market. Let's look at them one at a time.

1. Attitude

A bad attitude regularly keeps talented sportscasters from getting great jobs. It's a *hidden* killer because most people aren't aware their frustration is evident to employers.

Here are three examples:

A. An unemployed sportscaster grew frustrated over his inability to return to the industry. He was great at getting interviews but failed miserably in those interviews because he didn't hide his frustration. He didn't realize it was evident in his tone and words.

B. A sportscaster caught the attention of an employer who liked his work. When they met in person, though, the sportscaster's "woe is me" attitude over his recent firing killed his candidacy.

C. A sportscaster was frustrated employers weren't "appreciating his ability." He started lashing out via email at people who didn't hire him—going so far as to call them names and question their integrity. Those emails quickly made their way through the industry. He hasn't worked in sportscasting since.

As tennis star Andre Agassi said in the old Nike TV commercials, "Attitude is everything."

You can improve your attitude.

1. Don't speak negatives.

Doing so only gives life to your frustrations and makes a poor impression on others. Bad thoughts become bad things.

2. Focus on positives.

Post a list on your bathroom mirror of the good things in your life and career. Practice an attitude of gratitude. Good thoughts become good things.

Just like a bad attitude can unknowingly make a negative impression on an employer, a good attitude will make a favorable impression. It might be the final step towards your next job.

2. Anger

The second of the twin killers in the job market is anger. Argh!!!! The sports broadcasting job market can be so frustrating!

A sportscaster shared this struggle with me via email:

"It's official. The team I interviewed with went in another direction. Smith was always going to be hard to beat. I stand by my anger that I was part of a dog and pony show that was always going to end up with Smith getting the job. How do I get past my anger?"

Anger is understandable because the job market is frustrating, but...

You must let go of it.

Anger impacts the attitude with which you pursue other jobs.

I know a sportscaster who's been repeatedly frustrated in the job market. He's a talented guy but is not achieving the heights he anticipated. His anger came through in cover letters, follow-up voicemails, and emails with employers.

He didn't realize it, but I saw his anger clear as day in the cover letters he shared.

Remember that, even with a failed application, and even if you feel like you went through a dog and pony show, you gained something from the process. You spoke to the employer and had the opportunity for them to get to know you.

The person who interviewed you may be in charge of hiring for another employer one day. You might get that job based on this failed experience.

WHY WORKING HARD ISN'T ENOUGH IN THE JOB MARKET

When veteran college basketball coach Josh Pastner was a high school senior, he mailed letters to every NCAA Division I basketball coach. He wanted to be a coach and sought a program to accept him as a player/coach-in-training. He heard back from just a small handful of folks; one was Lute Olson at the University of Arizona. Pastner spent four years in Tucson as an end-of-the-bench player, then became a graduate assistant and went on to a long career as a Division I head coach.

Many sports broadcasters approach the job market much like Pastner approached looking for a school. They send demos and resumes to countless employers, hoping to at least hear back from one. What works for aspiring basketball coaches, though, rarely works for sportscasters.

You might be working hard in the sports broadcasting job market, but are you working smart?

There is a BIG difference.

Working hard is:

Sending your demo, resume, and a form letter to 50 employers hoping someone gets back to you.

Working smart is:

- Targeting a manageable list of 15 or 20 employers
- Customizing your cover letters based on your research of each employer
- Crafting customized demos when appropriate (This is critical when applying for sports talk host and update anchor jobs outside your market).
- Following up consistently and creatively with each employer.
- Building relationships with people who can help you with your search.

Working smart requires more time and effort than working hard. That is why the payoff is often great for people who do it.

STAY POSITIVE DURING A PROLONGED JOB SEARCH

A sports talk host once called me because he was considering quitting. He had introduced himself to the right people. He built relationships. He improved his craft. Yet, he was repeatedly frustrated in his attempt to move to a larger market.

During our call, I reminded the person that those who get to the top in sports broadcasting aren't always the most talented. They are the ones who persevered. Four months later, a large market radio station hired this individual as a host and programming assistant. He went from doing a daily show as a part-time employee and barely making any money to being a host in a large market with a full-time salary and benefits.

He earned his dream job because he stuck with it.

To stay confident in your job search, do something daily to earn your next job.

Progress breeds confidence. **You'll feel better when you feel like you're moving forward.**

One example of proactivity in the job market is the referral request we explained in Chapter 1: Career Advancement. Contact someone you know and ask for their advice on how to advance in the industry. At the end of the conversation, ask for three more people they can refer you to for a similar discussion.

The point is to do something every day.

Keep a calendar of things you will do:

- Submit applications
- Cold contact
- Follow up
- Connect with friends and colleagues
- Thank you notes
- Clean up your resume
- Update your demo

Use your calendar to track what you've done and what you are going to do. It will keep you on task. It will keep you moving forward.

Steady progress in your job search will increase your confidence and, ultimately, your results.

PURSUING DIVISION I PLAY-BY-PLAY

UNDERSTAND THE CHALLENGE OF LANDING A DI PLAY-BY-PLAY JOB

Among the most highly sought-after positions in sports broadcasting is being the football and basketball voice at an NCAA Division I university. At the time of this publication, there are 134 such positions. You only need one of them. Sounds easy, right? As Bugs Bunny would say, "Uhhhh...not so fast."

Yes, there are 134 positions, but turnover is slow because once a person lands one of those destination job gems, they don't want to leave. The other thing that makes landing one of 134 harder than it might seem is that five multimedia rights holders—Learfield, PlayFly, Van Wagner College, Legends, and JMI—control most of those schools. Instead of needing to impress just one of 134 organizations, you have just five to convince to hire you.

Making a full-court shot is easier if you have 134 tries versus five.

Fortunately, there are things you can do to increase your chances of scoring—to give yourself a half-court shot instead of a full-court attempt.

THREE TRAITS EMPLOYERS VALUE WHEN HIRING A VOICE

A Division I play-by-play job will open in most years.

Elite broadcasting ability is certainly a prerequisite for the positions. However, universities also look for other personal and professional characteristics when hiring the voice of an athletic program.

Here are three intangibles that universities value:

1. Likability

You will be the team's face on the air and in the community. Confidence, likability, approachability, and an even-keeled demeanor are important.

Your mic is still "on" when you are out in public—even though you aren't broadcasting over the air. You can't be grumpy when a fan approaches you in the grocery store, wanting to talk about the football team.

Other folks who must like you include:

- Coaches. Broadcasters have been fired because they didn't get along with a head coach.
- Administrators. Getting along with the person who signs your check is always good.
- Boosters. They often carry more weight than athletic directors.
- Fans. As an ambassador of the program, you will be speaking at Lions and Kiwanis Clubs, schools, pep rallies, and other community events.

2. Maturity

Maturity is more about moral conduct and common sense than age.

I've seen play-by-play folks get in trouble for being too honest about the home team, hanging out with players, not knowing their place on the airplane or bus, getting drunk in public, and conducting themselves in other ways that their spouses would not approve of.

Again, you are representing the university on and off the air.

3. Enthusiasm

Every minute you are on the air or in the community, you are selling the athletic program to advertisers, ticket buyers, other fans, and recruits.

It's easy to be enthusiastic about winning programs. Great play-by-play broadcasters, though, make lesser programs sound fabulous.

The traits of likability, maturity, and enthusiasm each relate to trust. Can the university trust you to represent them? Make sure the answer is yes.

How to Make the Jump to Division I

If you were starving and needed to catch a fish, would you fish in a lake with more than 130 fish, or would you fish in a lake with just five fish?

Unfortunately, trying to land a Division I football/basketball play-by-play job is like fishing in a lake with just five fish and hundreds of people trying to catch it. As mentioned, five companies manage most of the schools.

You must accept that landing a DI job is only minimally within your control.

Earning a prime college gig is overwhelmingly about luck and relationships. If you are willing to accept this reality, then keep reading. You can increase the chance that Lady Luck will smile upon you by controlling these seven variables:

1. Become an elite person.

The people who get Division I play-by-play jobs are passionate about their craft, focused, determined, and relentless. They are also great people. They are well-connected, know how to build relationships, and have influential people going to bat for them. They present themselves well, not just in the interview process but also in life.

Work to grow out of your shell if you're shy and reserved.

Another part of being an elite person is presenting yourself well physically. Take care to dress nicely. It doesn't mean you must wear suits everywhere, but dress neatly—especially at work. Put some gel in your hair and style it a bit. Be elite inside and out.

2. Develop your reputation.

Be known as a good person, easy to work with, diligent, polite, and likable. Work beyond your job description, never say no to opportunity, and treat people with kindness and respect. When a DI job does come open, especially in your region, you'll want many people eager to go to bat for you.

3. Build relationships.

Play-by-play success is more about who you know than what you know. Build relationships with sports broadcasting executives and talent at local radio stations, TV stations, and universities. You'll want their support when a local opportunity opens.

Also, build relationships with the broadcasters and athletic directors in your conference, broadcasters you admire throughout the country, employers, and everybody!

When a DI job opens for which you want to apply, you'll have people who will eagerly reach out to the employer on your behalf.

Employers prefer to hire people they know or who come recommended to them.

4. Meet hiring managers.

It can be difficult to meet hiring managers, but they're not confined to their offices. Hiring managers appear at industry conferences, sporting events, and other places. Find out where they are going to be, then be there.

However you do it, meet people so they can put a face and a personality with your name, resume, and demo.

5. Develop your skills.

Always improve. Get as many reps as you can, self-critique, and ask people who are already doing DI play-by-play for feedback.

6. Be patient.

You don't go from doing high school games in Broken Arrow to being the Voice of the Sooners. There is usually at least one intermediate step at a smaller college or university. The play-by-play job market rarely unfolds on our desired timeline, so stick with it, stay focused, and be determined.

There are three additional things to remember when pursuing a DI gig:

- "Writing the press release" matters. A university must be able to sell you to their fans.
- Alums always have an advantage.
- Many DI jobs outside the major conferences are part-time. You'll have to find something else to help pay your bills.

AN ALTERNATE ROUTE TO DI PLAY-BY-PLAY

Neil Price's 2017 move from women's basketball and baseball voice at the University of Kentucky to the football and men's basketball job at Mississippi State alerted me to a developing trend: You no longer have to be the football/basketball voice of a college program to get the same job at a Division I school. Doing baseball and men's or women's basketball at a major university can be an alternate route.

Additional schools that have hired a football/men's basketball voice who was not doing football at their prior school are:

- Nebraska: Hired Kyle Crooks to be the voice of Huskers football. Crooks had been calling Florida Gators women's basketball, softball, and soccer.
- Georgia Tech: Hired Andy Demetra, who was doing men's basketball and baseball at South Carolina.
- Nevada: John Ramey was doing baseball and Olympic sports at UCLA.
- Toledo: Hired University of Iowa women's basketball and baseball voice Brent Balbinot.

- East Carolina: Hired Duke women's basketball and baseball voice Chris Edwards (though he resigned shortly thereafter).

These events prompted someone to ask me, "What gets me closer to a DI football/basketball job, doing those sports at an FCS school or women's basketball and baseball for a Power 4?"

It is easier for someone to get a major college gig if they are doing women's basketball and baseball at a Power 5. One reason is that the basketball/baseball voices are developing major conference connections that can help them. In these positions, you are getting to know the same people who can open doors for you as you would if you were doing football and men's basketball at that school. The MSU AD who hired Price was the ex-baseball coach of the UK team that Price covered.

The second reason it's easier to get a DI football/basketball job if you are doing DI women's basketball is that it's easier to sell a new voice to the alumni when that voice is coming from a major university. MSU fans didn't care that Price was calling women's basketball. It was enough that he was coming from the University of Kentucky. It was the same with Ramey. Nevada fans were bursting with pride that their new voice had been at UCLA for 10 years.

Schools still value football broadcasting experience. However, many value a big-name employer on their new hire's resume even more.

YOUR TIMELINE FOR BECOMING A DI-CALIBER BROADCASTER

A young play-by-play announcer is doing Division II football and basketball in the northern U.S. He wants to know, "How long before I'm considered a Division I caliber broadcaster?"

There is no timetable for reaching the top. Your rate of improvement is up to YOU.

What are you doing to get better?

We all have the same 168 hours in a week. Some people turn those into network play-by-play or a Power 4 job, while others stay stuck calling high school games in Sheboygan.

The way you invest your 168 hours will determine when you're ready for a DI job.

It's up to you.

GENERAL

CONSIDER INTENT BEFORE ACCEPTING A JOB OFFER

A sportscaster I know quit three jobs within fourteen months of graduating college. Each job was a highly coveted position that received dozens of applicants. None of the three, though, moved him appreciably closer to his goal of television play-by-play.

Our friend has all the ability in the world. What he lacks is intent.

This person didn't know what he wanted from each job. You have no direction without intent or purpose, whether it's the job market, career, or life.

Consider intent when deciding whether to accept a job offer.

Why are you taking this job? How does it move your career forward? How does it get you closer to your long-term goals?

Understanding how a job opportunity will benefit you in the long run makes it easier to decide if it is in your short-term best interest.

FEELING WANTED IS NOT A GOOD REASON TO SAY YES

There are many good reasons not to accept a sportscasting job offer. You might easily overlook one of them if an offer is incredibly tempting.

I wanted to be a sports broadcaster since high school. Two years into my first job doing news and sports for a radio station in McPherson, KS, a station up the road in Salina asked me to be their news director. I nearly accepted the position even though it didn't include sports.

Salina seemed like a step up because it was larger than McPherson. The bigger reason I almost took it was because it felt good to be wanted.

After several days of deliberation, I turned down the opportunity. Thank goodness.

Had I accepted the job, I may never have ended up working at the sports radio station in my hometown of San Diego. I may never have learned sports talk show hosting, been the San Diego Chargers Radio Network host, had a show on ESPN Radio Network, or done TV play-by-play.

I almost missed all that simply because it felt good to be wanted.

A friend of mine is a radio sports broadcaster and station manager. He earns a healthy salary for his market. A local TV station asked him to work for them in a position that would have slashed his salary, didn't include sports, and didn't move him closer to his career goals. Still, he nearly accepted it because it felt good to be wanted. In hindsight, he's glad he stayed put.

Being wanted is flattering and sometimes intoxicating. By itself, though, it isn't a good enough reason to accept a job that will influence the course of your career.

BEWARE OF SPORTSCASTING FOOL'S GOLD

A sportscaster I know was facing a tough decision.

He said, "A startup company in my home state is offering me play-by-play for high school games on social media platforms and the possibility of my own show. There is also the possibility of broadcasting college football and basketball. They're offering $14,000 more than I currently make, and they tell me they have financial backers. The ability to do play-by-play for college sports excites me but I'm nervous about joining a startup."

He wondered how to evaluate the merits of a high-risk, high-reward opportunity.

Here are three important considerations:

1. Beware of startups.

Be leery even of startups that look ultra promising or like can't-miss. As I mentioned earlier, I was the first talent hire for a group starting a national cable TV network devoted to football. It was before the NFL Network, ESPNU, or any conference network.

This startup network had huge plans. I hosted their weekly radio segment for free for three years because they convinced me my big payday was coming. They sold their vision so convincingly that my wife and I bought stock in the company and encouraged family and friends to do the same.

Three years later, in August 2003, the TV channel finally launched. Four months later, it ran out of money and was off the air forever. The company never fully paid many employees.

2. Beware of "possibilities."

Maybe you've been told something like this:

- We can't pay you at the start, but we hope to be able to eventually
- We hope to be able to give you a raise after we syndicate the program
- We plan to launch the show on cable TV soon, and you will be the host
- You'll be the Afternoon Drive host after we get the station on the air. Right now, though, we need you to sell.
- This new podcast network is going to be huge. When it launches, you will be our featured show. For now, though,

> we need you to recruit folks who will pay to be on our network.

Here's another example: Several years ago, a company wanted to partner with STAA. They were recruiting folks nationwide to record recaps of major college football and basketball games. The employer would pay the reporter when they brought a certain amount of social media traffic to their stories. However, the minimum amount of traffic required for compensation was unrealistic. I said no to the partnership–I told them their setup seemed like a sham. They were insistent I wasn't giving them enough credit. I still said no; I didn't want to share an opportunity with our members that I didn't believe would pan out.

Nine months later, that company was out of business. It was another example of big hopes and dreams not coming to fruition.

In the example of our friend who considered returning to his home state, there was the *possibility* he would get to do college football and a *chance* he would get to broadcast college basketball.

Never make career decisions based on possibles and maybes. They mostly never come to fruition because if the company could pull them off, they would do so at startup.

It doesn't mean you can't root for those plans to become reality. Just don't commit to them until they do.

3. Ask about funding.

When considering joining a startup, ask where the money is coming from that will pay your salary. It's outstanding if it's from advanced advertising sales. Advertising is a recurring revenue stream.

However, if it's from startup funds, that money will run out, and the chance they can continue to pay you without ad revenue evaporates.

If you are still excited after removing maybes, possibilities, and "hope to's" from the equation, a job is worth considering. Be careful, though, not to be distracted by fool's gold based on hopes and plans.

Turn Three Job Market Frustrations into Advantages

Anyone who has applied for sports broadcasting jobs has experienced some degree of frustration. If it makes you feel better, the things that annoy you also annoy others.

Here are three common job market frustrations and how to make the best of them:

1. EEO posts

For job seekers, EEO means many position descriptions are published when there isn't an opening. The employer has either already filled the position or never had a position available.

Some employers publish the same position description every three months but never make a corresponding hire. Two corporations are so notorious for this that we rarely even post their "openings" on our job board anymore.

One time, I posted a sports radio position in the STAA forums. I then posted a follow-up comment along the lines of, "This is likely an EEO post. Don't get your hopes up." The station program director immediately emailed me to tell me the opening was legit. I replied that I wrote what I did because he didn't hire anyone the last time they posted the position.

They didn't hire anyone this time, either.

How to make the most of possible EEO posts: Apply anyway. You'd hate to miss out if it turns out to be a legitimate opportunity.

2. Applying to Human Resources

This is usually another result of EEO posts. Sending your demo and resume to the Human Resources Director is like putting a message into a bottle and throwing it into the ocean. You wonder if the actual decision-maker is ever going to see it.

How to make the most of applying to HR: When instructed to apply through HR, also send your application directly to the decision-maker. The decision maker is usually the program director at a radio station, the news director at a TV station, an executive producer at a regional TV network, or the general manager of a team.

3. Local hires

Many employers prefer hiring talent who knows the history of the local teams. That's understandable, especially in sports radio. Still, if an employer knows they will hire locally, it would be nice if they didn't solicit applications nationally. It wastes people's time.

I know an employer who always hires locally. Still, he feigns interest in out-of-town candidates—even for part-time positions—gets their hopes up, then tells them at the end of the process that he wanted to make a local hire. Considering the employer's preference all along was to hire locally, it was disrespectful to applicants to put them through the charade.

How to make the most of employers preferring to hire locally: Demonstrate you can instantly sound local by customizing your demo for the market to which you are applying.

KEYS TO STAYING PATIENT IN THE JOB MARKET

Every time STAA works with Learfield to fill a play-by-play opening, I invariably hear from several people who are stunned they didn't get an interview. Some of the surprise stems from entitlement or ego, but much is rooted in impatience.

Here are three keys to help you stay patient in the sports broadcasting job market:

1. Stay busy helping yourself.

Strategic activity equals energy, motivation, and confidence. One example is staying in contact with industry acquaintances. Keep them updated on your career and ask what they are hearing about possible job opportunities.

2. Always be working on your craft.

Study your work, listen to others, and ask for critiques.

3. Hone your job market approach.

Sharpen your demo, refine your resume, study the art of writing cover letters, and how to present those items to employers. Also read the information in this book about how to follow up your applications cleverly.

In short, always be improving.

PERSONALITY IS MORE IMPORTANT THAN POLISH

"They're strong, but they all sound the same." A network television executive told that to an agent who had presented a group of sportscasters.

The sportscasting job market underwent a seismic shift in the late 2010s: personality over polish.

Personality matters, both on-air and off. Employers and agents want to see that you're personable and sharing yourself on social media. They want sportscasters who are well-rounded and conversational.

Being too polished on-air can be a negative. You don't want to sound scripted.

The first thing many employers and agents do when considering whether to hire or sign someone is to check the candidate's social media following. How engaging and engaged is this person?

Here are examples of sportscasters with on-air personality, social media personality, or both.

- Ian Eagle, CBS
- Noah Eagle, NBC
- Don Orsillo, Padres
- Steven Nelson, Dodgers
- Dianna Russini, ESPN
- 2023 STAA Jim Nantz Award Winner Carlo Jiménez of the Clippers
- 2020 STAA Jim Nantz Award Winner Scotty Gange of KUSA Denver

- 2019 STAA Jim Nantz Award Winner Drew Carter of the Boston Celtics

They're all polished because polish is essential. But personality is even more critical.

DEFINE AND PROTECT YOUR PERSONAL BRAND

Apple, Costco and Nike are big brands with great reputations.

You, too, are a brand. What's your reputation?

The first thing an employer does when your resume hits their desk is Google you. They can instantly know your age, where you grew up, your mother's identity, and your arrest record. Employers can also see what you did in college, bad pictures, weddings, etc.

Protect your brand by controlling these two things:

1. Your behavior

Don't do stupid stuff that will forever top the search results when anyone Googles your name. The worst thing you can do for your brand is to muddy it up. You never want murky waters surrounding your name.

Employers are slow to hire folks with checkered pasts because the new hire reflects them.

2. Your internet presence

Having a personal website and LinkedIn page increases the chance the first things that come up in searches for your name are messages you control.

If you have a website, make sure it looks professional. Hire someone to clean it up if necessary. It's an investment in your brand. How your site looks and how you present yourself shows employers that you care.

You are your own best advocate. You represent your brand.

When an employer hires you, you are a reflection of them.

Make sure the reflection is a good one.

DON'T PANIC—ASK QUESTIONS WHEN STARTING A NEW JOB

When KNGL/KBBE in McPherson, KS, hired me for my first full-time radio job, I felt like I had been named to the NFL Pro Bowl. I was talented enough to be selected from among the other applicants, my future seemed endlessly bright, and I was fired up.

Then came my first morning on the job. Queue the sound of squealing breaks.

As I sat down at the typewriter (yes–a typewriter. It was 1989) in the newsroom, I almost a) wet myself, b) cried. What the H was I supposed to do now?!? The feeling of being a future sportscasting Hall of Famer I had experienced just one week earlier was a distant memory.

I was overwhelmed.

Fortunately, I figured things out quickly enough to work there for the next three years.

Here are two top tips for starting a new job:

1. Don't panic when you feel overwhelmed at the start.

The feeling of overwhelm happens to everyone. You'll learn your responsibilities and find your routine faster than you think. Probably much faster.

2. Ask questions.

Ask co-workers questions about how to do things. Don't ever feel like you're being a bother. Your co-workers will respect your desire to do things correctly and efficiently.

You were smart enough to get hired and you're smart enough to figure things out. But keep a fresh set of undergarments handy, just in case.

FIVE WAYS TO MAKE A GREAT FIRST IMPRESSION AT WORK

As mentioned, Day One at my first radio job after college was nerve-wracking. I was a San Diego kid in small-town Kansas, less than six months out of school. I worried the staff would see me as an inexperienced outsider.

Here are five things you can do to endear yourself to new co-workers quickly:

1. Bring donuts.

Bring them for the staff on your first day. It's hard not to like someone who just gave you a chocolate old-fashioned.

2. Read the bios of your co-workers.

What you learn on the station website will come up organically in conversation; they'll appreciate you taking the time to get to know them.

3. Be a team player.

When you see something that needs to be done, do it, even if it isn't in your position description.

4. Treat everyone well.

Be professional towards everyone, from the general manager to news and program directors, stage managers, and interns. You'll build your reputation quickly.

5. Be easy to work with.

Don't be demanding and don't expect preferential treatment.

Doing these things will ensure you are a rock star from Day One in your new workplace.

SOLIDIFY YOUR NEW JOB MARKET STRATEGY

You now have the knowledge to combine with your skills and experience to make a splash in the job market. Some final thoughts:

1. You hire you.

A former sports radio program director in Chicago said, "I don't hire you. You hire you." In other words, you'll get out of the job market exactly what you put into it. Working smart in the job market takes more time than simply working hard. The payoff is landing the job that advances your sportscasting career. Few things are more worth your investment of time.

2. Results take time.

It's sometimes difficult to invest in things that don't have an immediate reward. If you graduated from college, it likely took at least four years to earn your degree. Fortunately, the sportscasting job market doesn't take nearly that long, but you should expect it to take at least three months. Exactly how long it takes is based on your ability and effort. Looking for a full-time job IS a full-time job. If you aren't attacking it several hours daily, ask yourself if you are truly giving it your best shot.

3. Be unafraid to ask for help.

If you aren't sure you are doing something right, don't risk doing it wrong and potentially miss opportunities. Ask for help so you can put your best foot forward.

4. Take action.

A plan without action is only a dream.

The summer before my first year of college, I was training to try out as a walk-on for the basketball team at Kansas State University. My dad gave me a t-shirt. Printed on the back was, "Somewhere, someone is working harder than you. When you meet them head-to-head, they will beat you." The same is true in the job market. Invest the time it takes to be great.

Outwork others in the job market and set the bar by which everyone else is measured. You can do it.

Chapter 3:

Performance

CONVERSATIONAL SPORTSCASTING: FOUR TIPS FOR SOUNDING NATURAL

Sometimes, I listen to the first demo tape I ever made. I was a sophomore at the Princeton of the Plains, Kansas State University. The cassette (yep–cassette) included sportscasts and live reports from K-State football games for various radio stations around the conference.

As I listened, I blushed with embarrassment. I was bad. The sportscasts sounded scripted and rehearsed because, well, they were scripted and rehearsed. Yikes.

These tips are for you if you want to sound natural and conversational instead of stilted and rehearsed:

1. Avoid using a radio voice.

You should sound the same on-air as off. Many times, when people change their voices to sound more professional on the mic, they end up sounding like a caricature of a broadcaster. Talk like you. If you're unsure what your conversational voice sounds like, record yourself in a phone conversation. Study it and strive to be that comfortable when you're on the air.

2. Use natural word choices.

Don't try to sound smarter or more formal just because you're on the air. Avoid unnatural vocabulary. For example, you are unlikely to tell a friend that one team defeated another. You would instead say they beat them, ripped them, or smoked them. Use natural vocabulary.

3. Pre-read your script.

Read sportscasts, sports talk monologues, and other scripts aloud to yourself; make edits where the words don't feel or sound natural.

4. Listen to yourself.

When you are on the air, listen to what you are saying. You will often open the door for yourself to make a funny quip or otherwise deviate from your script or train of thought. Spontaneity makes you sound conversational. When you finish the spontaneous comment, return to the script. It's like being on the freeway. You can get off here and there. Just be sure to get back on so you eventually reach your destination.

Please excuse me now. I'm going to crush my old demo cassettes.

THREE TIPS FOR MASTERING YOUR VOICE AS AN INSTRUMENT

Vin Scully could have made as much money reading bedtime stories as doing play-by-play. If you've not heard the former Dodger great, listen online. Note how beautifully he used his voice as an instrument.

It's the single most challenging aspect of sports broadcasting to master.

These three tips will help you use your voice as an instrument:

1. Use all five gears.

Varying pacing and energy are especially applicable for play-by-play folks. Think of your voice as the transmission in a car. You don't always drive in one gear. Third gear may be the main gear for your play-by-play, but you can sometimes go lower when the action slows down. Other times, you want to go to fourth or fifth gear on big plays. But stop short of screaming.

2. Practice the 1-2-3-4-5 scale.

Here is a simple exercise to help you find your gears. Count from one to five, increasing your energy with each number. One is your delivery when you wake up in the morning; five is what you sound like if you win the lottery. Three—third gear—is where you should call most of your play-by-play. Four and five are your big play gears.

3. Use dramatic pauses.

You don't immediately know if the kick will be good when toe meets leather on a 50-yard field goal attempt. There is a dramatic pause when you're on the edge of your seat, wondering if it will split the uprights. Same with a big 3-point shot in basketball. It's not, "Shoots. Gooood!" No. The ball spins towards the basket for a moment.

Duplicate the pauses of the football tumbling through the air and the basketball floating towards the hoop by pausing. Ex: "3-pointer...Nails it!"

There will never be another Vin Scully, but mastering your voice as an instrument will help you sound your best.

TWO TECHNIQUES FOR FINE-TUNING YOUR DELIVERY

A mentor told a broadcaster doing play-by-play for high school sports to work on his pacing and energy. He asked me how to do that.

Here are two quick tips:

1. Read children's books.

One great way to hone your delivery, especially inflections, is by reading children's books aloud. The authors write in short, simple sentences with many adjectives—just like your play-by-play should be.

Harold and the Purple Crayon is my favorite for this purpose. Whatever book you choose, read it with the same animation as though you are reading to a child. You'll also develop a feel for pacing, pausing, and emphasis that will work for you on air.

2. Let your enjoyment show.

Some broadcasters struggle to sound excited without being over the top. The best way to increase your energy is to put your love for sports and broadcasting into your delivery. When someone gives you a surprise gift, you use a different voice than if you were telling someone their dog died. Some broadcasters get too caught up in trying to sound "professional."

Screw professional. Sound personable. And smile when you speak. You can hear a smile on the air.

VARY YOUR VOCABULARY TO IMPROVE YOUR PERFORMANCE

"No good!" is a phrase many play-by-play broadcasters use repeatedly on missed shots in basketball. Similarly common is "Over to" when a player passes to a teammate. You'll often hear both phrases dozens of times in a broadcast.

Mix it up. **Varying your vocabulary makes for a more entertaining and intelligent broadcast.** Creating vocabulary lists for each sport you broadcast is a great way to do it.

Compiling play-by-play vocabulary lists is as easy as 1-2-3:

1. Write down favorite descriptive words and phrases you are already using.

2. Add to the list words and phrases you hear other broadcasters using.

3. Add further by searching online for play-by-play vocabulary lists. Some great ones are available for free at staatalent.com/free-tools.

Elevate your broadcasting by improving your vocabulary.

Improve your on-camera performance

In my senior year at Kansas State University, I took a storytelling class from a wonderful woman named Charlotte McFarland. The purpose was to develop spontaneity and on-camera performance.

The local cable TV station filmed our class doing our final storytelling performances. When I watched my segment air the next week I thought, "You sure are a handsome guy, Jon." My second thought was, "I love the pink paisley shirt." My third thought was, "Dude, you have no camera presence. You look nervous, you look scared, you look reserved, and you're mumbling." So, I went about trying to fix those things.

I don't know if I've improved much, but here are some top tips for improving your on-camera performance.

1. Self-critique.

You'll notice things like mumbling and not looking into the camera —mistakes I made that you can fix yourself.

2. Seek critiques.

Other people will offer suggestions on things you're not noticing.

3. Talk with your face.

Study other sportscasters and actors. Note nuances in delivery and facial expressions. If they are surprised by something, you'll see wide eyes. You might see raised eyebrows and a downturned grin if they're amused.

Learn to use facial expressions to help convey the emotions that accompany what you are talking about.

4. Improve your writing.

"The Day You Became a Better Writer" is a blog post from Scott Adams, creator of the Dilbert comic. It's the best 90 seconds you'll invest in self-improvement today. Being a better writer will improve your on-camera TV performance.

Knowing these tips would have helped me a ton when I was in Mrs. McFarland's class. Oh well—at least I looked good in pink paisley.

Use Kobe Bryant's Example to Inspire Through Stories

Kobe Bryant was asked about his post-career plans when he retired from the NBA. He replied that he wanted to write books and make documentaries.

He said he wanted to inspire through stories.

Everybody loves stories. It begins in childhood with bedtime stories, and we never really outgrow it.

You can use stories to distinguish your sportscasting.

Sprinkle stories into your broadcasting if you're a play-by-play voice. People universally recognize baseball as a storyteller's medium, but broadcasters can also sprinkle stories into other sports.

Sports talk radio and podcast hosts: use a story in every monologue segment of your show. Your listeners think you have the coolest job. Take them behind the scenes of things you've done, seen, or heard.

If you are a TV sports anchor, use stories in your broadcast. You don't have as much time in a two-minute sportscast as a twelve-minute sports talk radio segment, but you have enough time for a story.

When you are interviewing someone, prompt your guest to tell stories. You can ask them directly to share a specific experience you know is interesting. Follow-up questions also lead to stories. If you ask two follow-ups on a single topic, the second question usually prompts your guest to share a story to illustrate their point.

Stories make for great broadcasts.

DON'T LET HATERS PROMPT YOU TO CHANGE YOUR STYLE

A college football broadcaster was in his second season with a new university. Message board trolls complained he wasn't enough of a homer on his broadcasts.

"The guy I replaced was not good with the fundamentals of play-by-play," he said. "He was a big-time homer who could complain about the officials and act like the game was a funeral if the team was losing. You could go 20 minutes without knowing the time, score, or even which teams were playing."

School officials were pleased with the new broadcaster. Still, he wondered, "Do I keep doing my thing and hope people get used to it, or should I be clearer that I root, root, root for the home team?"

My advice: stay with what got you there.

I would have crumbled when I was hosting on ESPN Radio Network if social media had been around. I would have ignored the supporters and catered to the critics. I would have changed what got me to ESPN to satisfy the haters.

That would have been wrong. Like the college football broadcaster, I got the ESPN job over dozens of other candidates because my bosses liked me and my work the most.

Stay with what got you hired.

People with positive opinions rarely share them. It is the negative nellies who go out of their way to criticize publicly. Trust me—their numbers are far less than they appear. It's like the Great Oz. He seemed mighty until the curtain was pulled back. It turned out he was a feeble old man.

One other thought specifically for our friend, the college football broadcaster: You are the voice of your school. It's nearly impossible you wouldn't pull for them to win. Consider the "professionally biased" approach. Fans know whom you want to win without you being a homer.

It's okay to sound more excited when your team does something well. You can still maintain journalistic integrity and professionalism.

INTERVIEWS ARE NOT CONVERSATIONS

I took great pride in my interviewing skills when I was on air. I wanted to be different and better than everyone else. At one point, I decided I could do that by making my interviews sound less like Q&A and more like conversations.

Big mistake.

Interviews are NOT conversations. **By definition, interviews are Q&A.** They are input/output. You input questions; your guest outputs answers.

If you hold conversations, it gives your guests too much leeway to go in whatever direction they want. Usually, it won't be the direction YOU want. Your guests will likely steer clear of subjects that make them uncomfortable. Plus, the guest is the star. More of them and less of you is a good thing.

Another reason conversations don't work is because they involve you making comments instead of asking questions. Guests often won't reply to comments, which brings the entire interview/conversation to an awkward, grinding halt.

Do these four things to distinguish yourself as an interviewer:

- Be prepared
- Have a plan—know what you want from the interview
- Ask open-ended questions
- Ask follow-ups based on being a good listener

It's funny—I wanted to have conversations to distinguish myself. It was only after realizing the error in that, though, that I could set myself apart.

KEYS TO GREAT PRE AND POSTGAME INTERVIEWS

One of the toughest challenges for sportscasters is pregame and postgame interviews. They can quickly become monotonous because you feel like you ask the same questions every broadcast.

Remember: **each interview should be different because each game is different.**

Here are some suggestions for keeping your interviews fresh. We'll address the postgame first because it will partially set up the following game's pregame interview.

Tips for postgame interviews:

- Keep two categories of notes during the game: team notes and player notes. Team notes are questions you can ask anyone on the team. Player notes are specific to an individual.
- Ask about turning points, big plays, and key injuries.
- Ask why the coach employed specific strategies. Ex: "Why did you change to zone defense in the third quarter?"
- Explore the ramifications of this win or loss.
- Ask about what's next for the team.

You might also keep a list of canned questions. You'll find a starter list in a moment.

Tips for pregame interviews:

- Start by asking two or three questions reviewing the previous game. They will likely be the topics you discussed in your previous postgame show.
- Ask what the team has stressed in practice since the last game.
- Ask about anything notable that has happened since the last game.
- Ask for injury updates.
- Ask for a scouting report on tonight's opponent.
- Ask about one or two of the opponent's key players. What do they do well, and how do you slow them down?
- If you played this opponent earlier in the season, briefly revisit something relevant about that game.

Be a good listener. Your best questions will usually be follow-ups to something your guest has said.

OFF-THE-SHELF QUESTIONS FOR POSTGAME INTERVIEWS

On ESPN Radio Network, I hated when my producer would pop into my headset to say, "We have so-and-so on from the baseball game. They just won 3-1."

Great. What am I supposed to ask the guy? I didn't see the game—I was on the air!

Tired of being caught off-guard, I put together some standard, off-the-shelf questions. Most aren't very insightful, but at least they can start the interview. From there, you can spontaneously ask more thoughtful questions based on the answers you receive.

Here are several ready-made postgame interview questions. Create variations of them for different sports:

- What was your approach to that critical at-bat?
- What pitch did you hit?
- What was the turning point?
- How have you hit against this pitcher in the past?
- How do you get ready to pinch hit?
- What kind of stuff did (your starting pitcher) have tonight?
- What is your scouting report on (the winning pitcher)?
- What wasn't working for (the opponent's starting pitcher)?
- When you get into a tense situation, what do you think about to stay relaxed?
- How did your coach feel at the half?
- When you were down X points, how did the team stay positive?
- Which of your teammates step into leadership roles in those situations?
- What has fueled your improvement as the season has progressed?
- How important is it to get on top early?
- (For a rookie) How do you adjust to the pro game's speed (or talent)?
- How do you compare the last few weeks to how your team started the season?

These questions at least serve as conversation starters. From there, **be an attentive listener and ask follow-ups based on your guests' replies**. Great interviewers respond to what they hear versus working exclusively from a list.

ADVICE FOR INTERVIEWING COACHES AFTER A LOSS

Imagine this scene: You're watching television. Somebody has just won a championship. There's confetti falling. A sportscaster stands atop a podium, interviewing the winning players and coaches. People are kissing the championship trophy. Pandemonium reigns. Then the network goes to commercial, comes back from break, and there's some poor sap standing in the silent corridor outside a locker room getting ready to interview the losing coach.

What do you do if the poor sap is you?

Maybe the situation I least wanted to find myself in during my career was interviewing a coach after a tough loss.

Here are some do's and don'ts to make interviewing a coach easier after a difficult game:

DO keep the interview shorter than usual. The coach doesn't want to be there, and neither do you. Still give your best, but keep it brief.

DO start by asking about positives. It will make it easier to ask your guest later about what didn't go so well.

DO ask, "What did you learn about your team? What did your team learn?" Those are thought-provoking questions; the coach may have already considered the answers during the game.

DO ask about feelings and emotions. Well, maybe. It's low-hanging fruit. You know the team feels crummy after the loss, but it can be interesting to hear your guest describe it in their own words. If you do it, be sure it's in a way that prompts reflection. Ex: What do you tell your team after a loss like this?

DON'T ask what happened or what went wrong. You will likely get some variation of, "I haven't watched the video yet."

DON'T offer your opinion on why the game went south or why they lost. Just ask the coach and let them share their opinion. The interview is not your time to show off your expertise.

Nobody likes interviewing a coach after a tough loss. Keeping these guidelines in mind will make it easier.

DON'T LOSE IT: SIX TIPS FOR TAKING CARE OF YOUR VOICE

There will be many times in your sportscasting career when your voice feels weak or tired. You may be doing play-by-play for multiple games each day at a tournament, hosting a three or four-hour talk show, or anchoring a sportscast when you are under the weather.

Here are six tips for taking care of your voice:

1. Rest

Get plenty of rest when you know your broadcasting schedule will get hectic. It's a logical point that shouldn't need to be said, but it's surprising how many broadcasters take it for granted.

2. Hydration

Sip water throughout your broadcast to keep your throat moist and your voice strong. I do stress sipping, though. It might be a while before you get a restroom break.

3. Avoid coffee and soda

Caffeine and soda pop can irritate your stomach and vocal cords; avoid drinking them while on the air. Soda's carbonation won't do you any favors, either.

4. Cough drops

Not just any cough drops, though. Sportscasters commonly recommend Fisherman's Friend and Hall's Breezers.

5. Earl Grey tea

Broadcasters with tired or scratchy voices swear by Earl Grey. The magic ingredient is oil extracted from the rind of bergamot oranges. It's WD40 for your vocal cords, and it tastes good.

6. Zarbee's Naturals cough syrup + mucus

Essentially, it is a mixture of ivy leaf and honey. Many sportscasters call it a game-changer for voice recovery.

Here are some other anecdotal suggestions shared with me by sportscasters over the years:

"Peppermint tea opens the throat and nose, and I find it soothing. I've been drinking it before every game, and it's actually cut down on my cough drop consumption during the broadcasts!"

"Dr. Tichenor's Peppermint Mouthwash mixed with water is magical. Saved me many a time."

"Honey and lemon juice combo on a spoon is soothing for a scratchy throat."

From Los Angeles Angels of Anaheim voice and former STAA member Wayne Randazzo:

"The first football game I ever called for ESPNU came on a day when I had no voice. A friend of a friend was a singer, and she suggested I drink aloe vera juice to soothe my throat. She said singers use that stuff all the time. It tastes disgusting, but it worked wonders as it got me through an overtime game. I couldn't talk during breaks, but I had enough to get through the broadcast. I drank half of a large bottle, and I haven't tasted it again since. In a real pinch, though, it does the job."

Finally, I once saw this on X:

"Lemon echinacea tea with a few tablespoons of honey before a game will have you good the entire broadcast."

One of these suggestions is bound to work for you.

Chapter 4:
Relationship Building

Relationship Building vs. Networking

Relationships, not resumes, move your sportscasting career forward.

Many people use the word networking to describe the process of meeting and getting to know people.

I prefer to call it relationship building.

Networking sounds like "what can you do for me." Relationship building is about "what can I do for you."

Several years ago, I received a surprise call from a friend. He asked if it would be helpful to me for him to promote an event I was hosting on his social media.

That is relationship building—what can I do for you?

Helping people is key to building relationships that will advance your career.

When my son was four, I told him, "To make a good friend, you must be a good friend."

Keep that in mind when building relationships in sports broadcasting.

Meet People in Person

A friend of mine is the best relationship builder I've met in sports broadcasting.

When CBS came to his town to telecast a PGA Tour event, he went to the production truck. He met Jim Nantz and an executive producer in charge of hiring talent.

When he visited a nearby city, he introduced himself to the athletic director at a local university and later got play-by-play opportunities with the school.

When he wanted to meet the hiring executives at a regional sports network, he told them he would be in their city and arranged a visit.

Relationship building with sportscasters and employers at the next level can seem challenging. It doesn't have to be.

Here are two ways to meet people in person who might lead you to future opportunities:

1. Go where they are.

Being close to someone you've not met in person is hard.

Like my friend who went to the production truck, the university, and the regional network office, go where the people you want to meet will be. Make time to meet someone when you're visiting a city for business or pleasure.

Don't just meet other sportscasters. Meet employers. If you travel for work, email the hiring manager of a local station and see if you can stop by for a few minutes to introduce yourself. You can also ask an employer for a tour of their facility. You will get to know each other during the tour and build the foundation for a strong relationship. An ESPN college football sideline reporter got her job after asking for a tour of ESPN's facilities.

Putting a face with a name can't be replaced. It's harder to forget someone you've met in person.

Many screen-centric Millennials won't take the face-to-face step, so doing it separates you. Most employers are older than you. They appreciate the value of personal interaction.

2. Attend industry events.

Only ambitious people go out of their way to attend industry events. They are precisely the people you want to know. And don't be shy. Put yourself out there—shake hands and kiss babies like a politician. (Disclaimer: don't *really* kiss babies. It's simply an old saying).

Rome wasn't built in a day, and one man didn't build it. The same is true for sportscasting careers. Nobody does it alone. Meet people in person. Build relationships.

IF YOU CAN'T MEET IN PERSON, MEET ONLINE

The digital age makes it relatively easy to connect with even the highest-profile people and offers multiple options:

1. Email

Email addresses for many sportscasters and employers are easy to find. If you can't find an address, it's often easy to figure out by looking at the addresses of other people within the company. Other tips for finding email addresses are explained in Chapter 2: Job Market.

2. Social media

Most everyone is there in one place or another.

3. Referral request technique

We discussed the referral request in-depth in the chapter on Career Advancement. Send an email to someone in the industry you respect. Ask if you can schedule a brief conversation regarding career advice. At the end of the call, ask who else they recommend you call for a similar discussion. When you contact those folks, you can then say you were referred to them by so-and-so.

The digital age has made the sportscasting world small and accessible to almost everyone. Take advantage of that to get ahead.

Here's what to say when connecting

Contacting people with a generic form message is the worst way to introduce yourself.

Instead, follow these helpful hints:

1. Connect personally

Sharing an alma mater, hometown, or something else obvious makes connecting easy. If not, maybe you find something they did or a place they've worked where you have a common connection.

If you're contacting an employer, dropping the name of a mutual acquaintance who already works there can give you instant credibility.

The point is to be a person, not an email. Sportscasting is a relationship business, so you need to connect on a personal level.

2. State why

If you don't have a prior connection with a person, explain what it is about them that you admire or respect.

3. Be genuine

Be sincere in your interest in the people you contact. Don't only talk shop with them. Get to know them personally.

Disingenuous relationship building is creepy—almost stalker-ish. If your only reason for contacting someone is to get ahead, don't do it.

4. Respect their time

When you contact someone, say in so many words, "I know you are busy. I understand if you don't have time to reply for several months, or maybe ever." They'll appreciate your respect for their time.

GROW NEW ACQUAINTANCES INTO RELATIONSHIPS

Meeting new people is easy. Developing relationships is hard.

After you've made a new acquaintance, you must maintain the relationship.

Here are suggestions for how to do it:

1. Send thank you cards.

Mail a handwritten card thanking someone for visiting with you or telling them how much you enjoyed the conversation. Few people send handwritten thank yous, so it stands out when you do. An email is nice, but a letter (a card) is better.

2. Stay in touch.

I guarantee my friend who visited the CBS production truck stays in touch with Jim Nantz, the executive producer, the athletic director, and the folks at the regional network. That's part of relationships—getting to know people and helping them get to know you.

Keep the people you meet updated on your career and congratulate them on their professional and personal successes.

3. Appeal to ego.

Everyone has a degree of ego. Stroke the egos of the people you meet by asking questions to make them feel clever. Ex: "Why did you make that lineup change? Oh wow, that's smart."

4. Stop by.

Reach out when you're in town. Swing by their office. Ask if they have some time for you. If you know them a bit, take them to lunch. Talk shop with them. Talk family. Exchange ideas. Strive to get to the point where you can help them.

5. Seek critique.
Every six months, ask if you can send a demo for critique. Think of all you accomplish by doing that. You're showing that person you want and can accept feedback, that you can grow, and that you value their opinion.

Those are traits of a person that anyone would want to help or hire.

6. Be patient.

Many people don't try to build relationships because the payoff is not usually immediate. Don't let that stop you. The delayed reward will be worth it.

7. Treat everyone like a VIP.

Sportscasting is a small industry. Treat everyone equally. You don't know who another person might know. Plus, a broadcasting intern in Class-A baseball today might be the voice of the Yankees tomorrow.

Building relationships is like nurturing the seeds for your future career success.

SEEK WAYS TO GIVE VALUE

A relationship is similar to a bank account. If you only take from the account, it will run dry. To prevent that, you must also give to the account.

It's called "relationship capital." Giving first earns you the right to ask for help later.

Many people tell me, "Jon, if I can ever do anything for you, let me know." I appreciate their willingness to help, but I don't know the skills and experiences that would allow them to assist.

Instead of telling someone you are willing to help, state *how* you can help.

Instead of asking, offer what you can give them. Two things you can give are assistance and feedback.

1. Assistance

Here are three examples of assistance you might offer employers:

- "The holidays are coming up. I know you'll have a lot of folks taking vacation. If you need someone to fill in on-air, I would gladly help."
- "I see a team from your community is participating in the tournament in my city next week. Please let me know if you need an on-site reporter for your station."
- "I notice your men's basketball team plays in my city the same day your football team is someplace else. If you need a play-by-play voice, I'm glad to help."

2. Feedback

- To a station: Offer thoughtful feedback on a program, podcast, or other content. Share what you enjoy and what stands out to you. If you have an idea that could enhance what they're doing, ask questions to learn more about their approach before offering suggestions. Your perspective can be valuable when shared respectfully and with genuine enthusiasm for their programming.
- To a network: If you work at a network affiliate, ask folks at the network what you can do at your local station or on your show or sportscast to help them. It could be to promote something the network is doing or to tell them how their national content is being received locally.

Giving to employers opens the door for relationship growth because the employer feels they need you, too.

When you give to others, it comes back to you double.

DIG YOUR WELL BEFORE YOU NEED WATER

A college play-by-play job opened. A broadcaster wanting to apply told me, "I worked with a guy who is close with the hiring manager at the university." I replied, "That's awesome! It's terrific to have an 'in.'"

Then he dropped a bomb.

"I haven't been in touch with this guy for a year and a half. Should I still ask for his help?"

This guy missed the boat.

Don't wait until you need a friend before building a friendship.

Make time to stay in touch.

Jordan Carruth was a student in the sports broadcasting class I taught at Palomar College near San Diego. Jordan stayed in touch after he graduated. He would call to ask how things were going and update me on his career. He would get my family San Diego State basketball tickets through his job at a local radio station. He kept in contact.

Ten years after graduating, Jordan ended up working for STAA.

When Brian Hanni was a student at the University of Kansas and later called women's basketball there, he developed a relationship with KU men's basketball coach Bill Self. Hanni stayed in touch with Coach Self after Hanni went to Texas Tech to call basketball. When the play-by-play job at KU opened, Bill Self was one of Brian Hanni's biggest supporters for the position. He got the job.

Staying in touch is the most valuable lesson I've learned in my sports broadcasting career.

I attended a conference—500 people gathered in a big ballroom. The speaker asked, "If you lost your job today, who would be 10 people you would contact for help?" He instructed everyone to write down the 10 names. Then he asked, "How long has it been since you've been in touch with each of them?"

There were murmurs throughout the crowd as most folks realized it had been a while.

The speaker next instructed, "Take your phones off silent and turn up the volume. I want you to text each of the 10 people. In your own words, tell them, 'I'm thinking of you. How are you?'"

What happened next was very cool. Almost immediately, sounds of ding, ding, ding filled the ballroom. People the audience hadn't been in touch with for some time started eagerly replying, happy to hear from their friends.

The point is to dig your well before you need water. Build relationships now.

An applicant for a Minor League Baseball job wanted to ask a Major League broadcaster he'd met to put in a good word for him. The problem was, he hadn't stayed in touch with the man. He hadn't dug his well and now when he needed water, the well was empty.

When employers ask me who might be a good fit for a position, the first people I think of are those who've stayed in touch.

There was once an opportunity to call a college basketball game in San Diego for Learfield. An STAA member who lives in the region, and who always stays in touch, was the first person I thought of. He got to do the game.

When a top 10 market sports radio PD needed someone, the first person I recommended was an STAA member who consistently stays in contact. He got an in-person interview for the position.

Staying in touch with people is the most valuable thing you can do for your sports broadcasting career.

Here is my challenge to you:

After you finish reading this, make your list of 10. Send a quick text to say hello. Set aside 30 minutes once per month to stay in touch with them so that when you need water, you've already dug the well.

STAY IN TOUCH WITH YOUR FORMER EMPLOYERS

A radio station laid off a sports talk host after eight years due to a budget crunch. Still, he stayed in touch with the station's program director.

Later, when the PD moved to a national network, he hired the host he'd let go several years earlier.

Stay in touch if you have a good relationship with a former employer. You never know when they might be able to help you in the future. Here are some ideas:

- Share when you see or hear something that reminds you of them.

- Congratulate them on their recent success.
- Wish them happy holidays.
- Thank them for the impact they have had on your career.
- Drop them a note to let them know you are thinking of them.
- Keep them updated on what you are doing.
- Wish them a happy birthday.

There is no need to strategize your message to an ex-boss. Let your heart guide you.

Sportscasting opportunities often come from people who trust you, not just people who know you.

Invest the time and effort to build relationships with people. You must be willing to put yourself out there. If you are naturally shy or introverted, fake it until you make it. You'll become what you act like.

Thousands of people want to work at the highest levels of sportscasting. You must outwork them and prove you are the person for the job.

RELATIONSHIPS TURNED INTO JOBS: SUCCESS STORIES

KNOWING THE HIRING MANAGER MADE THE DIFFERENCE

Dominic Miranda could teach a master class on building sports broadcasting relationships. Professional friendships were key to landing his first job as a sports reporter at WTHI-TV in Terre Haute, IN.

"As I was searching for jobs my senior year at DePauw University, I was looking anywhere and everywhere for job postings," Miranda recalls. "I started utilizing STAA's service in January 2019, and the constant job leads were extremely helpful. That's where I first saw the position in Terre Haute."

Fortunately, Miranda had already contacted two people at the station before the job opened. One of them was the person in charge of hiring air talent.

"The News Director, Susan Dinkel, graduated from DePauw so she was a part of my alumni networking outreach I did my senior year," Miranda recalls. "The Sports Director, Rick Semler, had recently won Indiana Sportscaster of the Year, and I just wanted him to see my reel. It was a perfect storm, and I was hired shortly after all this had transpired."

The WTHI staffers were far from the only people to whom Miranda introduced himself. "I had also reached out to almost 100 DePauw alumni and multiple Indianapolis sports personalities," he recalls. "There's nothing to lose when you humble yourself and ask for help from people who are successful in the industry. More times than not, they are extremely willing to help a young sportscaster."

Among the folks Miranda met through his relationship-building efforts were Indiana Pacers Radio Voice Mark Boyle, Pacers TV Voice Chris Denari, and veteran Indianapolis sportscaster Greg Rakestraw.

"Not only did I receive invaluable guidance and advice from these individuals, but two of them also made calls to Terre Haute on my behalf," says Miranda.

PERSISTENCE PAID OFF AFTER TWO YEARS

Josh Hess' acceptance of a Broadcasting and Media Relations Assistant position with minor league baseball's Dayton Dragons was almost two years in the making.

Hess' story featured several relationship-building strategies sportscasting job seekers everywhere would be wise to employ.

Here is his story in his words:

"The summer prior to my senior year, when I was calling games for the Falmouth Commodores on the Cape, I sent out emails with tapes every day to college and minor league broadcasters. While many of these tapes went unanswered, I got a critique from Tom Nichols, Dayton's number one [broadcaster]. He mentioned Dayton may have an opening at the time, but since it was a full-season gig and I still had one more year at Syracuse, I knew I wouldn't be considered.

"Fast forward one year [immediately after graduating]. I was still sending out multiple emails every day looking for critiques from experienced broadcasters and any openings they may have. Even though Dayton never went public [with their opening], I knew some other Syracuse grads had been the number two there, and Tom gave me great feedback [last year]. So, I reached out before the position was officially open.

"While pursuing the position, I stayed in touch with Tom as much as possible. One thing my dad has told me for years is to keep track of when you first meet/contact someone and what the topic of conversation is. I first contacted Dayton in late October and continued to follow up regularly until it came time to schedule an interview.

"Even after the interview, I stayed in touch. When Tom emailed me asking how my overall search was going, I was honest, telling him I had been talking with other teams to see what positions were available. Everyone in this industry knows two things about a job search: how competitive it is to find a job, and you can't put all your eggs in one basket. So, even though Tom knew I was talking with other teams, I continued to show interest in the position as much as I could."

Hess employed several relationship-building strategies: introducing himself, staying in touch, and making notes about conversations. These seemingly small things added up to his next opportunity.

COLLEGE CONTACT PAYS OFF YEARS LATER

Craig Hoffman's story perfectly illustrates how to advance a sportscasting career through relationship building. It's about how he landed at the Washington Redskins flagship station as their Redskins beat reporter.

He earned the job through a contact he made several years prior.

"My new program director, Dan Zampillo, and I had met years ago when he was at Sirius in New York," Hoffman recalls. "I don't remember specifically the first time I met Dan, but I wouldn't be surprised if it were when I was in NYC covering the Big East Tournament during my senior year in college."

Hoffman says the "human connection" he made with Zampillo helped him land the D.C. job. **"When someone feels invested in your success, they're more likely to help you achieve it."**

CHAPTER 5:

PROFESSIONAL DEVELOPMENT

GET UNSTUCK

My career was in neutral when I worked at XTRA Sports 690 in San Diego in the mid-90s. I felt stuck. Years later, I realized I wasn't stuck. I just didn't want to leave my hometown.

Is your sportscasting career really stuck?

Many sportscasters think they have been in the same place for longer than they want because they are the victims of circumstance.

Not true.

There are no victims of circumstance because the power to change your circumstance is yours.

If you feel "stuck," honestly evaluate how you are doing in these three areas:

1. Skills

Are you good enough for the positions to which you aspire? The job market is the ultimate scoreboard. If you aren't hearing back from employers, work to improve your craft.

Many sportscasting jobs include non-broadcasting responsibilities (social media, video shooting, editing, sales, etc). Make sure you are constantly honing existing skills and learning new ones.

2. Knowledge

Learn more about the sportscasting industry. For example, can you name the five largest broadcasting corporations in the United States? How about the broadcast rights holders for most major university athletics programs? Be a student of the industry.

Learn how to build meaningful relationships within broadcasting and stay current on industry trends.

3. Attitude

The enemy of a great career is a bad attitude. Skill only takes you so far. Promotions usually go to talented people who work well with others and treat people respectfully.

Remember that you have the power to change your circumstances.

It is easier to stay where we feel "stuck" than to tackle the unknown of moving to a new job. However, the challenges of a new job might be what you need to set yourself free.

THE REALITY OF OVERNIGHT SUCCESS STORIES

In Deion Sanders' Pro Football Hall of Fame induction speech, he recalled that when he went from Florida State to the NFL, people called him an overnight success. His response was he had been playing football since he was seven—that his overnight success was 13 years in the making.

There is no such thing as overnight success.

Kyle Crooks spent eight years broadcasting University of Florida women's basketball, softball and soccer. His goal, though, was to be the lead football and men's basketball voice at a major university but he didn't have a big-time football demo. Instead of lamenting his circumstance, Crooks regularly recorded mock broadcasts while sitting in an empty press box booth at Gators football games. He even prepared spotting boards as though his broadcast would be heard by masses of Gators faithful. A segment from one of those "mock casts" helped him land the job as the voice of the legendary football program at the University of Nebraska.

When I started hosting Weekend AllNight on ESPN Radio in 1999, some people said I was an overnight success. They said, "I've never heard of this guy. Where did he come from?"

Those people didn't know about the three years I spent doing news, calling play-by-play for high schools and small colleges, and hosting coaches' shows at the Wendy's restaurant on North Main Street in McPherson, KS. They didn't know about the six years I invested doing talk shows and sports updates for $13 an hour at XTRA Sports 690 in San Diego. They also didn't know that during that time, I coached basketball, worked as a fitness trainer, cleaned carpets, and washed cars to pay the bills.

Everyone loves the "overnight" success story. Many of us would love to have the perks of success without slogging through the work. Folks don't want to acknowledge the years of dedication you are working through to succeed.

You may sometimes feel alone. You may have family or friends who don't support your sportscasting career. Even if you don't personally know someone with a parallel career, know they're out there. Others share the struggles and sacrifices you are enduring in pursuit of your goals.

You are not walking alone. Many others have already navigated the path you are traveling and have found their ultimate career success. Instead of dwelling on the negative and getting stuck in a downward spiral of complaining, use your hardships to drive you forward.

You are smart. You can do it. And when you do, you can sit back and smile when someone calls you an overnight success.

14 ACTIONABLE TIPS FOR SPORTSCASTING CAREER GROWTH

A young broadcaster doing high school and small college play-by-play contacted me. He aspires to be the voice of a pro team, but he's concerned with the amount of job market competition.

"I am really dedicated to becoming a pro broadcaster, but it's a bit intimidating to hear how many people are applying to jobs nowadays," he admitted. "I get a bit anxious."

Understandable and not uncommon. Keep in mind, though, that you control your future. Keep taking steps towards your goals. Productivity decreases anxiety.

Here are 14 actionable tips to ensure you are moving forward in your sportscasting career:

1. Self-critique your work.

Spend 20 minutes weekly critiquing your work. Doing so with a critical ear is the fastest way to improve. Guaranteed. You will hear things no one else does and be your harshest critic.

If you are a play-by-play broadcaster or sports talk host, use the STAA Play-by-Play and Sports Talk Pyramids to guide your self-evaluation. They are available in the appendix of this book.

2. Seek critique from others.

Solicit feedback on your work from folks ahead of you in the industry. You can't fix what you don't know is broken.

3. Study others.

You can pick up things from sportscasters everywhere, from large markets to small ones. Listen to others for ideas, words, phrases, and techniques.

4. Update your demo.

Your recent stuff should be your best, so ensure it is on your demo. And do so now. You'd hate to be unprepared when a golden opportunity unexpectedly arises.

5. Tighten your resume.

Read in this book about what makes an effective sportscasting resume, and tweak yours accordingly. Be sure your experience, not your education, is the first section of your resume.

6. Improve your cover letters.

If you have been sending form letters into the job market, now is the time to promise yourself that you are going to start customizing your letters to the position for which you are applying. Again, read this book for in-depth cover letter suggestions.

7. Do something differently.

Stop doing the same things if you are stuck in a rut. Tweak your job market approach. Tweak your on-air work. Break out of your shell. Be more outgoing. Attend an industry event. If you're grumpy or negative, change your attitude. Whatever—find something to do differently.

Changing one thing might take you from bad to good, good to great, or great to outstanding. One change could lead to a bigger job or a better market.

7. Read daily.

I got this advice in a book from Mark Cuban. The information that can help make you great is available to everyone, yet most people don't read it. Learn more about sportscasting and the industry through books, blogs, videos, and internet articles.

You are trying to accomplish something that many other people have already achieved. Tap into their wisdom. Learn from their successes and failures to get where you want to go faster. Mark Cuban tries to read for one hour every day.

8. Listen to podcasts.

Turn your car into a classroom. There are many podcasts featuring sportscasters who have already navigated the trail you're on. Listen to them to benefit from their wisdom and accelerate your growth.

9. Read about industry trends.

Visit industry websites. Stay current with what's going on.

10. Attend seminars.

Go where opportunities, and the people who create them, are. You aren't likely to run into sports broadcasting employers and other influential people at your local Starbucks. Go where they are. You'll also learn ideas that will motivate and invigorate.

11. Introduce yourself to new people.

The more people you know, the more help you can get.

12. Find a mentor.

Identify someone who's been where you want to go. Take the person to lunch once a month. Learn how they got where they are. Learn how they think. Follow their examples and advice. Even the best athletes have coaches and trainers.

13. Build your team.

We all have people we lean on in challenging times. Think about who those people are in your life, then use them to help you with important career decisions. It is likely that not all of your team members will be in sports broadcasting. My team includes my wife, dad, sister, and a couple of broadcasting friends. The people who know you best will keep you moving in the right direction.

14. Be grateful.

Have an attitude of gratitude. When you appreciate what you have, more good things will come.

Talent alone won't advance your career. There are many talented sports broadcasters. **Moving up in the industry is about consistently doing things your competition is unwilling to do.**

Do them to separate yourself.

WATCH THE CLOCK TO BECOME A GREAT SPORTSCASTER

The following email is one of my favorites I have received from a sportscaster:

"I'm starting to make more time to get better. I recently announced my retirement from video games because I was making that a bigger priority. The more I studied my work, the more I realized that my second season of play-by-play for high school football was a sophomore slump.

"I don't want to struggle again. The only way to make that happen is to practice. Video games will no longer eat up that valuable time."

So smart.

When you engage in an activity, ask yourself, "If I say yes to this, what am I saying no to?"

This guy was saying yes to video games, which meant he was saying no to investing time to improve his career or prep for his next broadcast.

Many say, "I'm too busy to improve my sportscasting."

Too busy is a comment of self-importance.

Everyone has the same 168 hours in a week. How do you spend them? Are you playing video games or otherwise wasting them?

Zendaya has the same 168 as you and me. Noah Eagle, Jayson Tatum, Selena Gomez, and Mr. Beast all have the same 168 hours per week as we do yet accomplish much more than most folks.

How often do you say the following to yourself about building your sportscasting career?

- I'd love to assemble a fabulous application for that job, but I don't have time.
- I'd love to freshen up my demo, but I don't have time.

- I'd love to write a great cover letter, but I don't have time.
- I'd love to self-critique my work, but I don't have time.
- I'd love to study other sportscasters, but don't have time.

One hundred sixty-eight hours in a week is a lot. **"I don't have time" really means "this isn't a high enough priority for me."**

It's not a matter of being too busy. It's a matter of how you choose to spend your time.

If you sincerely want to create more time for advancing your career, here are some simple time management tips with big payoffs:

1. Write it down

Write down how you spend your days hour by hour for one week. You'll find the areas of waste.

2. Reset the alarm

Wake up 15 minutes earlier and go to bed 15 minutes later. You'll have another 3-1/2 productive hours weekly to devote to advancing your career.

3. Prioritize

What's more helpful to your career—*Game of Thrones*, Xbox, going out Saturday night, or updating your demo? If you want to be great, you'll make the time to do what's important. Prioritize your life so career responsibilities come ahead of recreational and social activities.

College Football Hall of Fame coach Lou Holtz organizes his priorities using the WIN formula—What's Important Now?

Applying that guideline to your time management will ensure you always put your best self on the air.

Put as much emphasis on making time to prep as you do making time to eat. One keeps your body thriving; the other does the same for your career.

4. Set a routine

Another key is to have a routine. When I broadcasted Arena League Football, I would make my spotting boards on Tuesdays and game notes on Wednesdays, then plug statistical info into my boards on Thursdays. Breaking large projects into several smaller tasks makes things manageable.

5. Keep lists

If your destination is greatness, a daily To-do list is your road map.

6. Work uninterrupted

It's counterproductive to stop your workflow every ten minutes to answer a text or email. Instead, set aside two or three blocks of time daily for correspondence. At the very least, ignore messages until you finish your current task. You'll find it easier and faster to write your cover letter and choose new stuff for your demo.

Turn off your phone, incoming notifications, or even your internet access to stay focused.

7. Consolidate trips

You'll save considerable time when running errands by merging two trips into one.

8. Find traffic jams

Critique your work when you are driving around town. (Unless you are a TV talent; don't critique while driving). You're not doing anything else when you're stuck in traffic, so turn off the radio and invest that time in polishing your craft.

Most sportscasters plan to be great until it is time to do what is required. A plan without action is just a dream. By following these simple suggestions, you'll create the time necessary to turn your plans into action.

PUT EGO ASIDE AND ACCEPT HELP

Sports Illustrated wrote a story many years ago about a huge defensive end at Baylor named Shawn Oakman. A quote from Baylor's coach, Art Briles, stood out:

"If you let people in, then you allow yourself to be helped."

The quote resonated with me because I often encounter sports broadcasters who don't allow themselves to be helped.

For example, STAA members receive detailed guidelines for how to write outstanding resumes and killer cover letters. These same job seekers will ask for advice when they don't hear back from employers. Glancing at their letters and resumes clearly shows they've ignored the advice.

The *San Diego Union-Tribune* once published a story about why people don't accept advice. One point it made was about ego. For some people, ego prevents them from accepting advice. They think they are doing everything right and refuse to consider the possibility they are not. I've been guilty of that throughout my life.

A common denominator among great leaders is they constantly seek better ways to do things.

They allow themselves to be helped.

The point of *Sports Illustrated's* story about Shawn Oakman is that he wasn't playing to his potential. Coach Briles intimated that Oakman could be an NFL star if he allowed himself to be helped.

If you feel stuck in your sportscasting career, Briles' advice might help you, too. Exercise my earlier advice about finding a mentor.

Seeking help will lead you to a bigger and brighter sportscasting future.

ADVANCE YOUR CAREER BY CHOOSING COURAGE OVER COMFORT

Years ago, a lawyer asked me to be an expert witness for his client, who sued CBS Radio over a non-compete clause. I'd never done such a thing. It made me nervous. Heck, it made me scared.

That's why I said yes.

Author Brené Brown is a former professor who studies courage. In a *60 Minutes* interview, she said, **"Choose courage over comfort. That's how you grow."**

When you're uneasy about something, it's often a sign that what you're about to do is good for you.

Here are a few ways you can choose courage over comfort in sportscasting:

1. Call a new sport.

If someone offers you the opportunity to broadcast lacrosse for the first time, do it.

2. Move to a larger market.

Moving can cause significant discomfort but will help you grow professionally and personally.

3. Share yourself on social media.

Though publicly sharing yourself might make you nervous, doing it is an important part of advancing a sportscasting career.

Instead of letting fear or anxiety keep you from doing hard things, embrace them. They move you forward. A person who is willing to be uncomfortable rises fastest.

Invest Your Free Time in Your Career

The San Diego Chargers had a player named Darren Carrington in the 1990s. His teammates called him "Prison Body" because he had washboard abs and was ripped. He looked like he'd been in prison, where he'd had nothing to do but work out.

He looked a lot like me.

Well, maybe not.

While I can't promise you washboard abs, I can share ways for you to strengthen your career by investing your free time wisely:

1. Trade critiques with a friend.

"You critique my work; I'll critique yours."

2. Study the stars in the sports broadcasting industry.

How do they do it? What questions do you have that can be answered by watching them? Take notes. Memory is not reliable. Plus, you can go back and review your notes again and again.

3. Practice your delivery.

Honing your delivery is something you can do whether you're a play-by-play broadcaster, sports-talk host, or sports anchor reporter. Read *Two Techniques for Fine-Tuning Your Delivery* in Chapter 3: Performance for suggestions on how to do this.

4. Create or update your website.

If you are a business or individual without a personal website, it's almost as if you don't exist. Use your free time to create a tool that will set you apart in the job market.

Free time is a luxury, but it's also a gift that can help you move up.

IMPROVE THROUGH INSTRUCTION, DEMONSTRATION, AND REPETITION

Legendary UCLA basketball coach John Wooden is my greatest mentor outside my father. I never met Coach Wooden, but he's profoundly influenced my life.

One thing I loved about Coach was his four-part method of teaching: instruction, demonstration, repetition, and correction.

Coach Wooden's methods will help you improve your sports broadcasting craft.

1. Instruction

There are several parts to this. Have teachers and mentors, people who can guide you. But choose them wisely. Only use people who have already been where you're trying to go.

A fabulous resource for instruction is the best sports broadcasting book ever written, *The Art of Sportscasting* by Tom Hedrick. It was published in 2000 but remains relevant and helpful today.

If you are a play-by-play broadcaster, another tool to improve your sportscasting craft is the STAA Play-by-Play Pyramid. If you're a sports talk host, use STAA's Sports Talk Pyramid for instruction. As previously mentioned, both pyramids are in the appendix of this book.

2. Demonstration

Demonstration should follow instruction. Listen to the people at the top of the industry. I like Kevin Harlan, Kevin Kugler, and John Sadak for play-by-play. They'll demonstrate how to do it.

3. Correction

Have people critique your work. Get unbiased ears on your demos for corrections and ensure the reps you are getting are of high quality.

4. Repetition

The fourth step of Coach Wooden's methods to improve your sportscasting craft is repetition. This means practice. If you can't get on-air reps, take your audio recorder to a game to practice. If the sport you want to practice isn't in season, watch a video, turn down the sound, and get your reps that way.

Also self-critique. As stated earlier, no one will be as hard on you as you are on yourself. You'll hear many little things that nobody else would notice that bother you.

Instruction, demonstration, correction, and repetition are The Fab Four to improve your sportscasting.

Respond Positively to Constructive Criticism

I sent my demo to a mentor early in my sportscasting career. It was under the guise of wanting feedback. Really, I wanted praise.

It crushed me when I didn't get it.

How do you respond when you get negative feedback about your work?

A veteran play-by-play broadcaster shared this email with me:

"I hear from a lot of young sports broadcasters. A whole bunch have never been told no or never stumbled or fallen. Once they get into this arena, they are stunned, in some ways, by almost everything.

"A sizable portion, though, after hearing a game on the radio or watching it on TV, think, 'Hey, that looks like a great, easy gig. You earn big bucks and are set for life.'

"They say they want critique. When you give it to them, they push back, are insulted, and go away. They do this even after I tell them "from the get-go that I'm going to be truthful, honest, and encouraging as I listen. Then reality sets in.

"The real ones buckle down, realizing this career is not easy—that it requires tons of prep and tons of work outside of the broadcast. And like anything else, they win sweet victories along the way as they move up. The others just stay jaundiced and go away."

How do you handle it when someone you've asked for a critique says you've got a lot of work to do?

Here are three things to consider about critiques:

1. Honesty can hurt.

The words stung when someone told me I wasn't the sportscasting prodigy I thought I was at 23, but they helped me grow. Honest critiques can hurt, but you will improve if you accept them constructively.

2. Don't make excuses.

Many people make excuses when told their work isn't as good as they thought. "I had a bad vantage point. I couldn't see the jersey numbers. I had a cold. It was the final game of the year with no one in the stands and both teams were playing out the string."

Don't make excuses. Own it when someone says you're not good enough. Improve.

3. Embrace the grind.

A sportscaster usually takes about 10 years to earn a comfortable living. **It's not always the most talented people who make it to the**

top. Those who persevere, even when receiving feedback about needed improvement, are the ones who go farthest.

USE CLEVER, ENTERTAINING MOMENTS TO STAND OUT

One of my pet peeves in sports broadcasting was the trend of TV sports anchors doing themed sportscasts to try to go viral on the internet. Yes, a sportscast featuring 20 Caddyshack references is clever and entertaining, but it's also a cheap publicity grab.

Great sportscasters are clever and entertaining each time they turn on the mic.

The subject of greatness brings me to Dan Cohen.

Dan was a sportscaster at WREX in Rockford, IL. Students at a high school basketball game scheduled a "Dress Up as Dan Cohen Night." Dan wore thick-rimmed glasses and had a cool, unique fashion sense. I was envious!

More notable is that Dan's audience loved him. That is why they honored Dan by being him for 90 minutes one night. (Search "High school students dress up as their favorite TV sportscaster; win home game.")

Great sportscasters don't need to beg for attention.

Great ones, like Dan Cohen, earn attention by being themselves and being consistently good each time they are on air.

SEVEN WAYS TO BE AS ENTERTAINING ON SOCIAL MEDIA AS ON AIR

An employer was interviewing a finalist for a play-by-play job. Things were going well until the employer asked the candidate how he used social media to promote his broadcasts. The candidate replied, "I Tweet (this was pre-X) a reminder about the start time for our broadcast."

End of answer. End of interview.

You must be social media savvy to work in sports broadcasting today. Here are seven suggestions for being as entertaining on social media as on air:

1. Go live

Go live on your platform of choice. Use a still photo accompanied by a 60-second voiceover to preview today's game. This "Pre Pregame Show" can feature players, coaches, dance team members, or starting lineups. Set up a two-shot on your iPad to interview someone. Broadcast batting practice or warm-ups. Be sure also to tease the start time of your broadcast. Sell it to advertisers.

2. Share the link

When posting your broadcast time on social media, always add a link where fans can listen. Make it easy for them to tune in.

3. Tag others

Tag people in your photos to move your message more quickly through your community. Remember to tag sponsors, too!

4. Pull back the curtain

Share pics of your preparation, your drive to the stadium, the inside of the press box, your spotting charts and game notes, the buffet in the media room, etc.

5. Take fans on the road

Shoot 10 seconds of video of you walking through the airport at 5 am. Share your view from the plane, out the window of your Uber, or from your hotel. Show the restaurant where you are eating dinner.

6. Interact in-game

Encourage listeners to post questions you'll answer during the game. Use a scheduling program to publish comments while you are on air.

7. Countdowns

Are there 19 days left until the start of the Padres season? Share a fact about Tony Gwynn, the most famous No. 19 in Padres history.

Sportscasters must be available to the public beyond when they are on-air. These suggestions will help you stay engaged with your audience, even when you aren't on the mic.

BE A LEADER TO MAXIMIZE YOUR JOB SECURITY

At one point in my sportscasting career, I had a boss who ruled through fear. He created an atmosphere where employees worried they were one mistake from losing their jobs. His leadership style was the direct opposite of that advocated by legendary coach John Wooden.

"Great leaders are always out in front with a banner rather than behind with a whip," said Wooden.

Being a leader is the best way to maximize your job security. And the great news is **you don't need a leadership title to be a leader within your station or organization.**

Here are 14 tips for being a leader in your workplace:

1. Make yourself a leader.

Leaders aren't appointed. They earn it.

2. Always be professional.

Treat others fairly and respectfully, and keep your cool when those around you are not.

3. Set an example.

Someone is constantly watching you, from team owners and general managers to station managers and interns.

4. Earn respect by doing, not dictating.

Get into the trenches with coworkers. Notice what needs to be done, then do it, even if it's not your job.

5. Be passionate about your job & station.

Fake it if you don't truly feel it. Convince others you have the best job in the world.

6. Dress for the job you want, not the job you have.

People will notice you as someone who holds themselves to a higher standard. You'll also carry yourself with more pride and confidence.

7. Communicate promptly.

The issue someone has contacted you about may be No. 12 on your priority list, but it might be Top 3 on theirs. They can't move forward until they hear back from you.

8. Be accountable.

Leaders own their mistakes, even when the error isn't their fault. A typical example is coaches taking responsibility for their team's poor performance when everyone knows the players laid the eggs.

9. Do what you say you'll do.

Be reliable.

10. Be a big thinker.

Don't settle for the status quo. Generate and implement ideas to move your team forward. The most valuable ideas will seem impossible to many but not to you.

11. Be willing to evolve.

The best time to make changes is when things are going well.

12. Be a friend.

Be approachable to coworkers who want to share ideas or frustrations.

13. Be a people builder.

Help coworkers feel good about themselves. If you must share a negative, sandwich it between a pair of positives.

14. Be willing to be led—and to learn.

Great leaders know they don't have all the answers. Stay open to others' perspectives and embrace ideas that move the organization forward, regardless of who comes up with it.

Being a leader will increase your job security and significantly increase your chance of promotion.

LET YOUR CONDUCT SPEAK FOR YOU

Is the way you are conducting yourself presenting the image you want?

A friend of mine was telling me about his experience in minor-league baseball. "I saw so many play-by-play broadcasters show up late, unprepared, and in t-shirts and jeans," he said. "You never know who is listening or watching you work. If you use the excuse that you'll be more professional in the Majors or a big market, you'll never get there."

Those comments couldn't be more right on. Look at them again:

"You never know who is listening or watching you work."

It's why Joe DiMaggio said he always played so hard—because someone might be watching him for the first time. The New York Knicks asked Tyler Murray to apply for their radio play-by-play job after an executive heard him broadcasting a college hockey game. Longtime Orlando TV sports anchor Christian Bruey was hired after the station's GM saw Bruey hosting a show on community television for his Minor League Baseball employer.

It's the same with you. Someone might be listening to or watching you for the first time. And it might be a potential employer.

You'll never reach the top if you say you'll be more professional once you get there.

That is one of my favorite job market quotes of all time.

Good habits aren't something you only start when you reach a certain level. They are the foundation that GET you to that level.

The way you conduct yourself says a lot about you. Make sure what you are saying is that you are a cut above the rest.

MANAGE BURNOUT BEFORE IT MANAGES YOU

A TV sportscaster sent this message to me. "I'm a one-person band at my station—sports anchoring and reporting. I'm wearing myself out to ensure I have plenty of local content each night. What can I do?"

I had two suggestions for her, one practical and the other mental.

1. Work in bulk to ease your burden

Batch producing works for both TV and radio reporting. Come up with several different stories surrounding a local team. Attend practice and interview coaches and players who can contribute to multiple stories. One trip, several packages. Look at the upcoming schedule for story ideas. Collect comments from your players and coaches discussing teams, coaches, and players they'll see in the coming weeks.

2. Daydream

When feeling especially tired or frustrated, envision yourself in your dream job for a few minutes in silence. Feel the excitement, accomplishment, and satisfaction that will come with that opportunity.

Remind yourself it is the reward of tomorrow for which you are grinding today.

Doing that will provide the energy and motivation for you to keep moving forward.

We grow most through trying times. Remind yourself of that when feeling especially challenged in your sportscasting career.

THINKING ABOUT GIVING UP YOUR SPORTSCASTING DREAM?

Someone came to me seeking encouragement not to give up his sports broadcasting dream. He was five years out of college, doing high school play-by-play on a small AM/FM combo in the Midwest. He thought for sure he'd be broadcasting college sports by this time. His parents and his new bride suggested he consider a career where he could earn more money.

Here is the four-part advice I gave him:

1. Be patient

Life and careers rarely unfold on our desired timelines.

2. Be ready.

Opportunity will present itself. The key is to be ready when it does. Preparation includes building a network of relationships within the industry—folks you can help in some way who, in turn, will want to help you.

3. Be proactive.

Opportunity will likely present itself faster when you seek it rather than wait for it. Contact friends in the industry to discover where unpublicized opportunities might be.

4. Choose your response to frustration.

We reap what we sow. Where you are today in your career is a reflection of past behavior. Where you are tomorrow will result from the decisions you make today.

Few people face truly unique challenges in building a sportscasting career. Most everyone starts in a small market. Everyone struggles at times to pay their bills. Everyone has felt overworked and underappreciated. Some folks crumble; others overcome.

We're all dealt the same hand. How you choose to play it will make a difference.

Nine Skills to Reinvent Yourself in the Sportscasting Industry

It is becoming increasingly rare to find full-time work doing just play-by-play, TV anchoring and reporting, or sports talk show hosting. You have to do more. If you can't or are unwilling, your career will suffer.

These nine skills will help you stay relevant in sportscasting:

1. Social media

Knowing how to post on X, Instagram, and TikTok is insufficient. The content you share must be compelling.

2. Video basics

Video is the preferred way to consume online content. You'll give yourself a significant edge in the job market if you can be comfortable on camera and learn how to frame, shoot, and edit great content.

Topping your list should be learning how to do Instagram Live and YouTube Live.

3. Website management & coding

At the least, you'll need to be able to upload and edit content on your employer's website. In the bigger picture, you should have a website featuring your demo and resume. WordPress, Squarespace, and Wix provide templates that make it relatively easy even for the un-tech savvy to build a website.

Learning basic HTML and CSS will also serve you well. There are plenty of websites that will teach you to code for free.

4. Media relations

Creating press releases, game notes, recaps, and stat packs is the primary part of most play-by-play jobs in minor league sports.

5. Software

Knowing audio and video editing, graphic design, and other software programs gives you a key advantage in the sportscasting job market. Learn programs like Audio Vault, Audacity, Adobe InDesign, Photoshop, Illustrator, Premiere, Audition, Final Cut Pro, News Edit, and Quark.

YouTube is a great place to learn.

6. Basic design principles

Simply knowing how to film and edit a video or create a graphic in Illustrator won't be enough to set you apart in the job market. Understanding fundamental design principles like balance, space, and color will help you create better videos and graphics for social media and websites.

7. Podcasting

Podcasting is a common part of sportscasting jobs. Start one to demonstrate you can do it and that you have the discipline to do it regularly. It will also help you stay relevant and make new industry connections.

8. Sales

You'll always have a job in sportscasting if you can sell. The best place to learn how to sell is inside a bookstore. Thousands of books about sales have been published, but only the best make it into bookstores. (The challenge today is finding a bookstore).

9. Production

Learn how to shade cameras, run cameras, run replay, do graphics, etc. Knowing how positions in the truck/studio/control room work helps when you are in front of the camera. Understanding your support team's roles helps you make their jobs easier. And the crew respects you more when you've been behind the scenes with them.

The sportscasting industry is constantly changing. You must be, too.

It's okay not to want to be a star

There's a music documentary that answers a question many sportscasters have:

Why have I not made it to the top?

20 Feet from Stardom is about backup singers in the music industry. Even though they are often as talented as the people for whom they're singing, they stay in the background, always 20 feet from the spotlight.

If someone is immensely talented at singing or sports broadcasting, what might keep them from getting to the top?

The singers in the documentary explain three reasons:

1. You're comfortable where you are.

Some folks are uncomfortable in the spotlight. Being center stage would take them out of their comfort zone.

As long as it's what you want, there is nothing wrong with staying out of the spotlight.

2. You don't want to be vulnerable to failure.

Some people's fear of "putting themselves out there" prevents them from selling themselves. Other times, it makes them uneasy about staying in touch and building relationships that lead to jobs. It's okay if that is your choice. But people who choose not to put themselves out there also choose not to be upwardly mobile.

3. You don't want to play the game.

Many singers remain backups because they are unwilling to play the game—they're unwilling to politic or suck up. Again, they make the choice, understanding if they don't play that game, they might never be front and center.

Many sportscasters say they want to be at the top yet are unwilling to invest the necessary effort into their craft or the job market.

That lack of effort is a symptom, not a cause. The cause may be rooted in being uncomfortable in the spotlight, too shy to put themselves out there, or unwilling to play the game.

A lot of great singers never take center stage by choice.

Many great sportscasters, too.

18 THINGS I WISH I HAD KNOWN AT 22

An aging pro athlete said, "Now that I'm old enough to know everything, I'm too old to use it." Here are some things I have learned over the years that younger readers might still be able to use:

- You don't know what you don't know.
- Relationship building is the fastest way to advance your career.

- Be clear about which team has the ball on a play-by-play broadcast.
- Good play-by-play is a story, not a narrative.
- The people you meet on the way up are the same ones you'll see on the way down.
- Employers notice the attention to detail.
- Team players generally go farther, faster.
- What's good for my station is also good for me.
- Landing a full-time radio sportscasting job in a major market is HARD.
- Play-by-play is largely a part-time industry.
- Entry-level sportscasting jobs DO pay as little as my mentors had warned me.
- I thought I knew everything, but I knew nothing.
- Programming at small market stations is vastly different than programming in large markets.
- My $18,000-a-year salary was unattractive to hot chicks.
- Being Howard Stern in McPherson, KS ticks off local listeners.
- Winning in the job market requires following up on your applications.
- Talent alone is not enough to make it to sports broadcasting's big-time.
- You'll eventually forget the frustrations of your first job and remember only the great stuff!

Embrace your journey. The journey lasts longer than the brief thrill of arriving at your destination.

Chapter 6:

Personal Growth

15 TRAITS THAT PREDICT SPORTSCASTING SUCCESS

Sports broadcasting employers must listen to someone's work for just 30 seconds to decide if they like it. Similarly, it takes just a few minutes of conversation to know if a person can have a long career in sports broadcasting.

Here are 15 traits that foretell sportscasting success:

1. Confidence

If you don't believe in yourself, nobody else will.

2. Inquisitiveness

When FOX TV sportscaster Joe Davis was an underclassman at Beloit College, he contacted sportscasters nationwide for answers to his questions.

3. Likability

Be easy to get along with, and someone folks enjoy being around.

4. Motivation

Identify your why—the reason you want to excel. That is your motivation.

5. Outgoingness

Be enthused to meet and talk to people. If it's not naturally your personality, fake it until you make it. You become what you act like. "The me I see is the me I'll be."

6. Proactivity

An aspiring sportscaster living in the Southern California desert would drive 2-3 hours to meet sportscasters, buy them coffee, ask questions, and get to know them. I was one of the people he visited. That broadcaster, Marco Peralta, ended up as the Spanish language voice of the Los Angeles Dodgers.

Don't wait for an opportunity. Create it.

7. Perseverance

Sportscasters who go farthest set a goal, draft a plan for getting there, and stay the course. They are undeterred. The loser says, "It's too hard; I can't do it." The winner says, "It's hard, but I'll find a way." **Perseverance is more important than talent.**

8. Big thinking

A student in my former sportscasting class got a Super Bowl head coach on our school's sports talk radio show just three nights before the coach's team played in the Big Game. Most coaches don't do radio for Los Angeles, New York, or Chicago stations three nights before the Super Bowl, yet this student got the coach on our campus station because he was determined. Big thinkers understand that "impossible" simply means it hasn't been done yet.

9. Relationship building

As you read in Chapter 4, relationships are the bridge between talent and opportunity.

10. Understanding of the industry

You should have industry awareness. That means knowing most sportscasters don't start in the NFL or at ESPN. It also means understanding the steps necessary to get where you want to go.

11. Responsibility

Do what you say you will do when you say you will do it.

12. Problem solving

Focus not on problems but on solutions.

13. Accountability

Don't make excuses, and don't blame others.

14. Maturity

Thinking and acting beyond your age. Some maturity comes only through life experience, but not all of it. Accelerate your maturity by actively seeking improvement in each area of this list.

15. Dress well

As mentioned earlier in this book, dress for the job you want not for the job you have.

People talk about the It Factor, the hard-to-define trait that allows someone to command attention when they walk into a room. Developing these traits will bring you the It Factor.

Talent is mandatory for going far in sports broadcasting. However, many folks are as talented as you. Developing these personality traits will set you apart and move you towards the top.

PRIORITIZE PERSONAL GROWTH OVER CAREER ADVANCEMENT

A sportscaster told me he was running out of perseverance and belief in himself. He wrote, "That feeling when you get rejected by a cute girl is the same feeling I've got over and over the past four or five years when I miss out on job opportunities."

As the message continued, it included such phrases as "Gut-wrenching pain; starting to fatigue; I feel it in the pit of my stomach; I just feel lost."

He added, "I'm sorry to sound so defeated. I've just been at this for a long time now, and I can see no end in sight."

I share the message because such thoughts are not unusual. I felt similarly in my own sports broadcasting career. When I was at ESPN Radio Network, I tried to get a second show on local radio. I was unsuccessful, even though I was a national host.

The key is to work less on your career and more on yourself; a healthy mind, body, and soul equals peak performance. Have a morning routine. Exercise your mind as well as your body. Express gratitude. Set the tone for a great day.

Seek inspiration to improve your attitude.

You will grow your sportscasting career proportionate to how you improve your attitude. As the great personal growth expert Zig Ziglar said, "Your attitude will determine your altitude."

SEEK INSPIRATION DAILY TO MOVE YOUR CAREER FORWARD

When STAA hosted its annual sports broadcasting seminar, attendees would leave brimming with enthusiasm for their careers. Everything they ever wanted to achieve seemed possible. Unfortunately, the enthusiasm dissipated for many attendees until it was eventually gone.

Here's the key: **Seeking inspiration is like bathing. You need to do it every day for it to have an impact.**

You can find motivation for your sportscasting career in many places—books, blogs, podcasts, videos, and conversations. I am a longtime mentee of Oprah Winfrey, Jim Rohn, Zig Ziglar, Napoleon Hill, and W. Clement Stone. John Wooden tops my list of virtual mentors. I've not met any of them, yet they've profoundly impacted my life.

Each of these mentors helps me improve my mindset, motivations, and how I do things.

We've already discussed books. Here are other sources of daily motivation and inspiration:

1. Podcasts

The choices are innumerable. Opt for ones that resonate with you. There are even many podcasts by sportscasters, for sportscasters.

2. Videos

I love videos about people's accomplishments, perseverance, determination, and triumphs.

3. TV Shows

The businessman in me loves watching *Shark Tank*. I got a lot of ideas from that show, as well as from *The Profit*, which aired on CNBC.

Find shows that resonate with you and keep you motivated.

4. Documentaries

Watch documentaries to fire you up or lend insight into the mindset behind accomplishment and achievement.

5. Movies

I especially lean on movies to fuel my mental toughness. For example, when I watch *The Junction Boys* and see what Bear Bryant put his Texas A&M players through, I feel more capable of handling my workout, even if it's a little painful or tiring.

Wherever you find inspiration, partake in it for 15 minutes daily, and you'll take a huge step ahead.

READ EVERY DAY TO STOKE YOUR SPORTSCASTING PASSION

As we shared in an earlier section, Mark Cuban reads for one hour daily.

Cuban recalls when he started as a software salesman, he knew nothing about what he was selling. He learned by reading instruction manuals. Then, when prospects had questions, he could answer them thoroughly and professionally.

Cuban outsold everyone and set himself on the way to riches.

Other software salespeople had access to the same manuals. Cuban says the difference is he invested the time to read them. He is one of many leaders who makes time to read daily.

I have observed on social media and through interaction with sportscasters that many dislike reading books. Wow—so many folks are missing out on treasure troves of information and advice that can be difference-makers in their careers!

Learning should be a lifelong endeavor. Highly motivated individuals in any industry make time to read. Yes, podcasts and articles can contain helpful information, but nothing matches the details and depth of books.

There are many ways to continue learning after you finish school. Reading is one of the best ways to continue growth.

Information is motivational fuel. Learning new ideas and techniques fires you up and helps advance your sports broadcasting career.

Many personal growth books and biographies exist about people overcoming challenges and achieving success. They all have great value. Choose something that resonates with you and read it.

Apply "Think and Grow Rich" to your sportscasting career

On his sports talk show, Radio Hall of Famer Jim Rome said that his dad made him read Napoleon Hill's classic personal growth book

Think and Grow Rich. Rome said every dad made his kid read it. I thought, "Not every dad because I've never heard of the book!"

Still, Rome read the book and he was doing okay, so I read it, too.

One chapter in *Think and Grow Rich* is about the essentials of leadership. I translated these essentials into six attributes of sportscasting success:

1. The habit of doing more than you're paid for

Work beyond your position description. Everyone in sportscasting is expendable, but you'll make yourself harder to replace by doing more than is required.

2. Pleasing personality

Be easy to get along with. Bob Costas has been renowned for it throughout his career.

3. Mastery of detail

You build something great when you consistently stack small things atop each other. Joe Davis used to transcribe his broadcasts to study his word choices.

4. Willingness to assume responsibility

Leaders are great at this. Say it is your fault when people in your charge make a mistake, even if it is not. If it is your fault, own up to it. You look foolish trying to deny it.

Everybody makes mistakes. Learn from and don't repeat them.

5. Cooperation

Get along with and help your coworkers. Pitch in when you see something that needs to be done, even if it's not your job.

6. Ability to organize

Many sportscasters say they wish they had time to do career-improving things but believe they're too busy. Saying you are too busy is an admission of inefficiency. If you want to build a great sportscasting career, you must develop the ability to organize your duties and time.

Working on your skills is necessary to move forward. More vital is working on yourself. These tips from *Think and Grow Rich* will help you do it.

LESSONS FROM A COACH THAT CAN BOOST YOUR CAREER

One of my favorite ESPN series was Being PJ Fleck. It was filmed in the months immediately after the always upbeat Fleck was named football coach at the University of Minnesota.

These eight Fleck-isms will help you improve your sports broadcasting career:

1. Own your happiness.

Happiness is a choice. You can fret and be grumpy that your career isn't yet where you want it to be, or you can choose to appreciate your job and accomplishments.

I wish this were my mindset when I worked at the old XTRA Sports 690 in San Diego. Instead of being grateful for having an on-air job at a major market all-sports station that hundreds of people would love to have had, I moped that I didn't have a daily show. My negativity kept me from being my best.

What a PITA I must have been to work with.

2. Find new ways to do things.

Old ways aren't always the best ways. The speed at which technology advances makes it easier than ever to reinvent the wheel. Find ways to increase the performance, efficiency, and time management of yourself and your station. Doing so will make you stand out.

3. Always be improving.

Constantly be striving to get better. Seek critiques. Self-critique. Read blogs. Listen to podcasts; study other sportscasters. If you aren't getting better, you're regressing.

4. Change your best.

Seek improvement relentlessly. Do it in the non-sportscasting areas of your life, too. Change your best regarding the speed at which you reply to correspondence, the gratitude you share with sports information directors who help you prep your broadcast, and your reputation among coworkers for being easy to work with.

5. Serve and give to others.

Be doing something for somebody else all the time. It is a great way to build lasting relationships within sports broadcasting. Don't ask others what they can do for you. Instead, do things for them.

One of the easiest and most valuable things you can do for another sportscaster is to connect them with someone who can be helpful to them.

You'll get what you want if you help enough other people get what they want.

6. Smiling is my favorite.

Smiling makes coworkers eager to be around you and makes you feel better. It's hard to feel negative when you have an ear-to-ear grin. Sportscaster Ian Eagle is great at this.

7. Don't allow yourself a threshold where you'll quit.

Most people have a point where they'll say, "Enough is enough." They'll stop cold-contacting employers after repeated rejection. They'll stop seeking improvement when it hasn't led them to a better job. They'll stop working their best when they feel unappreciated by their employer.

I've been guilty of the latter. Not only did I keep myself from being my best, but I kept my coworkers from being their best because I was the weakest link in the chain. How selfish I was.

8. Row the boat.

PJ's most well-known mantra. When adversity hits, put your oar back in the water and keep rowing. Persevere. Again, don't allow yourself a threshold where you'll quit.

These fundamental tenants serve B.J. Fleck well in his coaching career. They'll do the same for your sportscasting endeavors.

TALK TO YOURSELF INSTEAD OF LISTENING TO YOURSELF

Former Philadelphia Eagle-turned-magician Jon Dorenbos wrote a book titled, *Life Is Magic: My Inspiring Journey from Tragedy to Self-Discovery*.

If you're unfamiliar with Jon's football career, perhaps you saw him on America's Got Talent. What makes his story unique is when Jon was about twelve years old, his father killed his mother. The book is about Jon's lifelong journey of forgiving his father and conquering the challenges of his unique life circumstances.

One of Jon's habits will be especially beneficial to sportscasters looking to advance their careers:

Talk to yourself instead of listening to yourself.

Our thoughts tend toward the negative. It's human nature. Even in my fourth year as a host on ESPN Radio Network, I often wondered, "How am I here? I'm not good enough to be here. Management will realize it any day now, and then I'll be finished."

What helped me was positive self-talk like that advocated by Jon Dorenbos. I changed my mindset when I recognized those negative thoughts by saying, "I am good enough to be here. I am a national-caliber sports talk radio host. I've prepared fifteen years for this opportunity."

A small dose of positive self-talk will re-orient your mindset.

It may sound like hocus pocus, but try it right now. Give yourself positive affirmation about your career: "I am good enough to be the voice of an NFL, NBA, or Major League Baseball team. I am good enough to have a career in sports broadcasting. I am talented, and I am well-prepared for my next opportunity."

Do it regularly, and the mindset will help you enjoy sportscasting success, just like it's helped Jon Dorenbos overcome and achieve.

APPLY OPRAH'S ATTITUDE OF GRATITUDE TO YOUR SPORTSCASTING

Another person I especially admire is Oprah Winfrey. She and Dorenbos both exude joy and gratitude.

Feeling gratitude is critical to experiencing joy. Here's why: **it's impossible to experience negative emotions like frustration, disappointment, or anger when feeling gratitude.**

Here are a few things you can do to feel grateful in your sportscasting journey:

1. Do like Oprah: Keep a gratitude journal

I started keeping a gratitude journal many years ago. I write in it daily, often about things I've done with my wife and son.

At the start of your day or before you go to bed, write down five things for which you're grateful. Some can be career-related, but they shouldn't all be. It might be as simple as a beautiful sunrise or chirping birds. Write down whatever makes you thankful. Your mindset will begin to change. It's like exercise. The more you exercise, the healthier you get. It's the same with feeling gratitude.

2. Mail hand written thank you cards to people who have impacted your life

It can be family members, friends, teachers, or people who have helped you advance your sportscasting career. Or it could be somebody you haven't had contact with for twenty years. Imagine the joy and happiness you'll bring them when they receive your heartfelt message of thanks. The act of writing the note will dramatically lift your spirit as well.

3. Wish something good for someone else

"I hope my friend crushes her broadcast tomorrow." Thinking kind thoughts for others helps fuel a positive attitude.

How will all this improve your sportscasting?

It's something we mentioned earlier in this chapter: more important than working on your career is working on yourself.

When you have the right mindset, you will approach the job market with a better attitude. You'll approach your interaction with prospective employers from a more positive place, and you will have a better attitude and outlook when you broadcast.

Have an attitude of gratitude. It will improve your sportscasting. I promise.

THE 90-DAY GRATITUDE CHALLENGE

Running STAA is a lot like being a bartender. Many people are comfortable sharing their career and life challenges with me. I appreciate their trust; they know anything they say to me in confidence stays with me.

I share this because many of the sportscasters I talk to are "glass half empty" people. New opportunities would come if they flipped their perspective and became grateful for what they have.

Frustrated in your job?

Be grateful you have a job to go to each day. I've made $18,000 per year, and I've been unemployed. $18,000 was more enjoyable.

Is it sometimes hard to get excited to go to work?

Be grateful you get paid to attend games you would want to attend anyway. When I earned $18,000 per year, many of my friends from Kansas State University earned twice as much. Several of them, though, didn't enjoy their jobs. They always asked me about my career—who I had seen in the Chargers press box or what Junior Seau and Tony Gwynn were like in person. What my job didn't pay me in money was compensated for with enjoyment and enthusiasm.

Frustrated you've been unable to take the next step in your career?

Be grateful daily that your current job provides opportunity to grow. While working as a weekend sports talk host in San Diego, I applied for a full-time job in Phoenix. I felt I had a great chance at landing the position. Ultimately, I didn't get the gig because I wasn't ready. I continued honing my craft, and ESPN Radio Network hired me the following year.

Disappointed you didn't get the job for which you interviewed?

Be grateful you are now squarely on that employer's radar. It may lead to a better opportunity. When one broadcaster finished runner-up for the play-by-play job at a major university, he could have thought, "Woe is me." Instead, he told friends how grateful he was to get to know the person in charge of hiring for Learfield Sports. Weeks later, when another major college job opened, Learfield hired this broadcaster.

There is no such thing as a perfect job. **Don't dwell on the things you don't like about your career; be grateful for all the positives.**

Here's my challenge to you:

For the next 90 days, express gratitude for your career every day. Either speak it or write it down. After 90 days, the shift in your mindset will be permanent. The new outlook will open doors in your career.

How a Gratitude Challenge Changed a Sportscaster's Perspective

Paul Bulkley once had a full-time sportscasting career. He called play-by-play for Weber State University, Dixie State College, and Salt Lake Community College. He'd also worked as a sports director and talk show host. Today, he's a full-time high school teacher who occasionally does play-by-play on the side.

Sometimes, Bulkley laments that he's no longer on-air full-time, But instead of regretting what he doesn't have, he's learning to appreciate what he does. Gratitude helped him make that shift.

When I first introduced the 90-Day Gratitude Challenge to sportscasters, the idea was simple: fake a positive attitude until it becomes natural, then watch your life improve. Bulkley accepted the challenge and began sharing his daily reflections in a thread on the STAA website.

Here's why he did it:

"I accepted the 90-Day Challenge to create some change in my life. I was at a point where I wanted to feel better about what I was doing in the classroom as well as in my career as a broadcaster."

Bulkley's challenge: balancing career and family.

The travel and relocation that come with sportscasting were manageable for Bulkley. But they were becoming tougher on his wife and their four children. He knew stepping away from full-time broadcasting was the right choice for his family. But that didn't make it easy.

"One of the most challenging things was letting go of my sportscasting career so I could become a teacher," recalls Bulkley. "I have not fully let my broadcasting career die, but it has taken a back burner so that I can provide for my family. Traveling and moving from one city to another has also been a challenge. With four children, it is not always easy for them or my wife to adjust."

The results:

Upon completing STAA's 90-Day Challenge, Bulkley gained a deeper sense of appreciation—for himself and for others.

"When you appreciate yourself, you have more value in yourself. In other words, you see yourself as more valuable to the group or organization; thus, you can place more value on others. It becomes a win-win situation.

"My mindset has been more positive and upbeat since I took on the 90-Day Challenge. I look for more ways to show appreciation towards others, and I feel better about myself because of it."

An STAA blog post later featured Bulkley as one of the success stories from the 90-Day Challenge. It wasn't about prestige—it was about possibility. That exposure never would have happened had he not taken the Challenge.

And now, his story has come full circle. Bulkley is in this book, too.

He concludes, "The Challenge helped me focus on doing what was best for my family rather than for me. It also helped me understand that I can be a great teacher and have my broadcasting career on the side."

EMBRACE SETBACKS TO ADVANCE YOUR CAREER

Did you know that embracing setbacks can help you grow your broadcasting career?

Here's a story to illustrate what I mean.

I once recorded a Facebook Live video. I was excited. I had excellent sportscasting content to share. I set up the camera nicely. The lighting was good. Everything was perfect.

So I thought.

The audio and video were unsynced when I watched the finished product. I was disappointed. I thought, "Oh, man. I did everything I could to make this good."

After a few moments, I realized I wasn't the first person this happened to. After a moment of research, I found and fixed the problem. I left the botched video on Facebook as an example of growth.

You must try new things to grow.

The more I used Facebook Live, the better I became. The same is true with things in your sportscasting career.

Years ago, I filled in on play-by-play for Washington State University. Their baseball team visited for a weekend series at San Diego State. On the Friday broadcast, I tried to sound like Vin Scully. When I listened to the recording on my drive home, I thought, "Wow, what a dope! You sound like a total moron."

Vin Scully is great at sounding like Vin Scully. I wasn't. But I learned from it. I tried something; it didn't work as planned, so I changed it. The Saturday and Sunday broadcasts were great.

What might you do differently on your next broadcast?

If you're a sports talk host, try using bullet points instead of scripting your monologue. For play-by-play, try increasing your energy. It might feel awkward at first, but try it if it's something you think you need to do.

If you're a sports update anchor, experiment with increased pacing. You can always go back to your previous style.

Don't be afraid of imperfection. The only way you will grow is by trying and tweaking. Perfection is the enemy of progress.

Fearlessly try new things. Any setbacks will be learning and growth opportunities.

Is Ego Holding You Back?

A sportscaster shared something that turned around his career: honest self-evaluation. It impacted his career more than reading books, attending seminars, and studying other sportscasters.
Humility helps us improve.

I thought I was pretty good when I hosted sports talk radio in San Diego. I was in my mid-20s, working in a top market. The funny thing is, as good as I thought I was, the industry didn't see me the same way. Whenever I applied for jobs, I never got a call back from employers. I realized how much I needed to improve after reviewing my work and humbling myself. Once I did, ESPN Radio called, and I hosted there for four years.

Sometimes, we avoid honest self-evaluation because we believe we are already good enough. Other times, we are afraid of the realization that we might not yet be as good as we think.

Think about that. **We often avoid self-evaluation because we fear the realization we might not be as good as we think.**

My sportscaster friend says honest self-evaluation improved his play-by-play. The same thing improved my talk show and advanced my career.

It will do the same for you.

Define the Line Between Personal and Professional Fulfillment

Chris McManus is wise beyond his years.

At 28 years old, McManus left his sports talk gig at ESPN Radio Syracuse. He hoped to find a job that provided a better balance between his professional and personal life.

"When I was just coming out of school, I thought that if you loved your job, nothing else really mattered," McManus told Syracuse.com. "But in the radio industry, you often have to move all over the country, and you might not have a permanent home until your 30s or 40s. When I was coming out of school, that sounded okay. At 28, you start to evaluate some of those things."

Finding where to draw the line between personal and professional fulfillment is a challenge that eventually confronts most sportscasters. Not only is the line in a different place for each person, but it usually moves as we get older. Things we value when we are younger can become less important as we enter new stages of life, like marriage and family.

One thing that makes finding the line easier is maturity. Ego often minimizes with age. **When ego gets small enough, it makes it easier to find fulfillment**, even if our careers aren't unfolding as we once imagined they would.

Chris McManus's choice wouldn't be right for everyone, but it was right for him. Huge props to Chris for having the wisdom to determine where to draw his line.

SIX TIPS FOR A HAPPY SPORTSCASTING HOME

You are a basketball play-by-play broadcaster. You're married and have at least one child who would love nothing more than for you to be at home to play with tonight. However, the team you broadcast for plays on the road in a post-season tournament. Lose, and you go home. Win, and you are spending another night in a Holiday Inn.

Your team wins. What do you hear in your child's voice when you tell him you aren't coming home for at least another day?

Sports broadcasting can be an incredible and fulfilling career. Like anything, though, there are challenges. Days or weeks away from family is difficult. Feeling like your spouse might think you aren't pulling your weight around the house or with the kids can strain a marriage.

What are you doing to cope?

The premise of this topic, and the following suggestions, comes from experiences shared with me by a friend who is the voice of an NCAA university. They were similar to comments I have heard from other sportscasters.

1. Establish a pre-road trip ritual.

Do your family's laundry and wash the dishes before leaving on an extended trip. Take those tasks off your spouse's plate so they can parent while you are away and not have those menial tasks hanging over their head. Radio host and author Dr. Laura Schlessinger once said that nothing makes a man more attractive to his wife than easing her burden. Perhaps the same applies in reverse. (Hey babe—where's the dish towel?!?!)

2. Establish a return ritual.

Agree with your spouse that, upon returning from a road trip, they will give you a morning to veg out—play with the kids, relax, sleep late—whatever you want and need to ease back into home life.

3. Make sacrifices.

Your spouse and kids sacrifice considerably in their loving support of you. Pay them back by giving them your time and undivided attention, even when tired.

4. Have a date night.

Make time for your significant other. Date nights are valuable to all couples—even more so when one-half of the couple is often away.

5. Unwind together.

Find things to do with your significant other—running, puzzles, movies, board games. It doesn't matter what, just so long as it's something.

6. Bring 'em along.

Invite your family to accompany you on a road trip. Some college athletic directors will allow an entire family on the charter to bowl games. Others will allow you to take a child to one road game per season. If that isn't the case, bring your family along at your expense once a year. (Be smart about where you invite them. The road trip to San Diego State is better than the one to Iowa State).

Acknowledging the burden your career sometimes puts on your family and doing things to ease it will help ensure your home remains happy.

ADVICE TO MY 30-YEAR OLD SELF

For part of my career at the old XTRA Sports 690 in San Diego, I cohosted a nightly show called The XTRA Sports Hour. It was like SportsCenter on the radio.

I was able to crank out creative scripts in a short time. I'd finish quickly and have an hour or more before airtime.

I would waste that hour.

I often went to the back office and talked to my now-wife on the telephone. Other times, I read or did who knows what.

When pondering the advice I would give my 30-year-old self, I thought of this story. It was a hard place to go. I'm not proud of that aspect of my 30-year-old self.

I was selfish. I was only in it for me. Instead of wasting that hour, I could have helped the other guys with their scripts. I could have helped record and cut audio for the show.

I didn't realize my selfishness was hurting my chances for advancement.

So, what advice would I give to my 30-year-old self?

Be a team player. You'll get what you want by helping enough other people get what they want.

Is the trash can full? Empty it, even if it's someone else's job.

Notice what needs to be done, and then do it, even if it's not your job.

Work beyond your position description.

A VINCE LOMBARDI QUOTE THAT CAN TURN AROUND YOUR CAREER

Vince Lombardi said, "The difference between a successful person and others is not a lack of knowledge. It is a lack of will."

I hear daily excuses from sportscasters trying to justify why they are stuck.

- "I don't have time for the extra things to stand out in the job market."
- "I don't have time for extra prep."
- "I don't have time to self-critique."
- "I don't know anyone who can review my work."
- "I can't meet people because of where I live."
- "I can't afford to attend that conference."

Review Lombardi's words again: **"The difference between a successful person and others is not a lack of knowledge. It is a lack of will."**

Success will be yours if you want it badly enough.

Chapter 7:
Mindset

SPORTSCASTING DOES NOT BELONG ON THIS LIST

Fact: Sports broadcasters earn less money than many other working professionals.

Fact: Sports broadcasters love going to work more than many other professionals.

I share these facts because, years ago, a now-defunct website published a list of the ten worst jobs. Broadcasting made the top five. Granted, the article listed "broadcasting," not "sports broadcasting," but still...

The article based the ratings on these four factors:

1. Environment: This includes includes physical demands, hazards, and proximity to danger.

2. Income: Average beginning, mid-career, and top incomes.

3. Outlook: Based upon unemployment data, potential employment, and salary growth.

4. Stress: Including deadlines, competitiveness, and how often your life is at risk. The website said about broadcasting stress: "For those who are able to find full-time work in broadcasting, success requires a high threshold for stress."

With these four factors as measuring sticks, it is easy to see why corrections officers and taxi drivers were among the top ten worst jobs. But broadcasting?

Let's look at the four factors realistically as they pertain to sportscasting:

Environment

A baseball ballpark is one of the most beautiful, safe, and wholesome settings where a person can work. Football, basketball, and hockey aren't far behind (unless you are covering a Raiders game, in which case, yes, you might be in danger).

Income

It's a fact that sports broadcasting salaries generally stink. You're lucky to earn your age.

However—and this is the most prominent place where the website blew it—the compensation for sports broadcasters cannot be measured only monetarily.

How many people earning $75,000 a year love going to work every day?

How many are paying top dollar for parking and admission to games sportscasters attend for free? How many would love to be in the locker room, get to know the players, attend practice, and sometimes be treated like a celebrity around town?

Outlook

Because of live streaming, opportunities for sports broadcasters have never been more abundant.

Stress

Every profession has deadlines to some degree. Every profession is competitive. Anyone who complains about the competitiveness of their chosen field should find courage. And as far as "how often your life is at risk,"—well, when was the last time you heard of a sportscaster dying on the job? It's not even a threat. Again, unless you are covering a Raiders game.

Most of the folks who read that website's list would love to have our sportscasting jobs.

10 AWESOME THINGS ABOUT BEING A SPORTSCASTER

Sports broadcasting is an awesome profession. As mentioned, many of your friends would love to have it. From that perspective, I assemble this list: "10 awesome things about being a sportscaster."

1. Getting paid to attend games you would be going to anyway.

2. Gaining perspective on the unbelievable athleticism of pro athletes that comes with sitting courtside.

3. Being inside the locker room after a big win.

4. Traveling to new cities.

5. Meeting new people who share your love for sports.

6. The beauty and history of minor league ballparks.

7. Getting to know athletes your friends only see on TV.

8. Free stuff, like food, books and shirts.

9. Watching high school athletes you've covered move onto the pros.

10. Veteran sportscasters eager to "pay it forward" are common.

Remember: an attitude of gratitude will advance your sportscasting career.

Is this also the reason you chose sportscasting?

Kobe Bryant said one thing he wanted to do after basketball was produce documentaries about successful people. He said he would first ask, "Why do you do what you do?"

Upon hearing that, I stopped to ask myself why I chose sportscasting as a career. The answer I have always told people is I wanted to get paid to go to games.

Kobe would have wanted me to go deeper if he featured me in one of his documentaries. Why did I want to go to games? Well, because I love the energy and athleticism of sports. I love watching people compete and achieve. I love the variety of emotions on display.

Being in a sports environment makes me happy.

That is why I chose sportscasting—not so I could go to games, but because doing so makes me happy.

During my career, I sometimes lamented that my monthly four-digit paycheck started with a one. I wish I reminded myself that I chose sports broadcasting because it made me happy.

Happiness. You can't put a price on it.

Am I good enough?

Am I good enough?

I get that question all the time. It's a common human insecurity.

Oprah Winfrey says when she finished recording episodes of her TV show, her guests would almost always ask, "How did I do?" It didn't matter if the guest was a housewife from Sheboygan or a Hollywood star; they always wanted to know, "Was I good enough?"

When I speak on college campuses, I often ask the professor, "How was it?" Knowing I crushed it, I still wondered, "Was I good enough?"

Don't worry about, "Am I good enough?" That comes from a place of comparison.

Focus on what you can control.

John Wooden rarely scouted opponents. Instead, he concentrated on making sure the Bruins did everything to the best of their ability. If they did, he knew they would be good enough most of the time.

Another thing to do if you wonder if you are good enough is to listen to the job market. It whispers to you.

If you're not hearing back from employers, the job market is whispering you need to improve your work or how you apply for jobs. If you are getting interviews without offers, the market is whispering that you need to change how you're interviewing.

Don't waste energy asking if you are good enough, worrying about what anyone else is doing, or comparing yourself to others. Comparison is the thief of joy. Instead, concentrate on making yourself the best you can be.

That will be good enough.

YOU MIGHT BE CLOSER TO YOUR GOALS THAN YOU THINK

A young sportscaster asked if there was ever a point in my sports broadcasting career when I doubted myself.

Of course there was! Doesn't every sportscaster experience that at least once? It wasn't my ability that I started to doubt as much as it was the chance I was ever going to get where I wanted to go.

My goal was to go as far as I could. I didn't care if it was play-by-play or sports talk show hosting. When I experienced my self-doubt in 1999, I had considerable experience in both.

At the start of '99, I was a sports update anchor and talk show host on XTRA Sports 690 in San Diego. I hosted weekends and mid-week fill-ins and regularly hosted the night show for many months. I even filled in several times for Jim Rome on his fledging radio network. However, we had an all-star talk lineup at XTRA, and I was never full-time.

My football, basketball, and baseball play-by-play experience were similarly extensive but also largely part-time.

My son and I enjoyed racing Hot Wheels. Seeing how far we could get them to go was always exciting. We didn't care which car went farthest—we just wanted to make one of them go as far as possible.

That is how I felt about my career ambition. I didn't care if it was NFL, NBA, MLB, or major college play-by-play or being a host on a network.

I just wanted to go far.

Just a few months into 1999—at the height of my self-doubt—my big break came. ESPN Radio Network needed a new host. They called my boss. Long story short, I got the gig.

I bring this up because there was a message I wish I had shared with the person who asked if I had ever doubted myself:

Trust in yourself. Many people quit without realizing how close they were to achieving their goals.

MOST OF YOUR SPORTSCASTING MEMORIES WON'T BE OF THE GAMES

A story was published years ago about former Montana Grizzlies voice Mick Holien. It described how Mick was selling a bunch of memorabilia he collected over his 31 seasons as the Voice of the Griz.

The story started me thinking about my favorite memories from my sportscasting career. My top two aren't even about on-air stuff.

1. Road trips with the Anaheim Piranhas

Traveling with the Arena Football team was the most fun I had in my radio career. There were countless memories: Sharing meals with players Sam Hernandez, Jai Hill, Skinny Culver, media relations guy Kurt Van Fossen, and others; golfing with Kurt on a crummy course outside Des Moines; a Saturday night out with kicker Ian Howfield; poolside in Phoenix with Coach Mike Hohensee; an awesome pregame meal in Des Moines; ordering three entrees at a greasy spoon in Milwaukee and eating them all; Disney World with Kurt and trainer David Chaffin; Church Street in Orlando; a weird gothic bar in Houston; a team staff member getting dropped at the side of the road by a woman he'd picked up; receiver Bryan Reeves getting me a second meal from the galley on the flight home from Houston. Too many more to list.

2. Camaraderie with my ESPN Radio crew

Pre-show prep and commercial breaks were always a blast. It was often the most entertaining stuff we did each night, on or off the air. Cutting up with our producer Jason McBride, board op Brian Fitzgerald, update anchors Damon Bruce (miscast as an update anchor; he turned out to be a better host than me!), and the late Neil Jackson. It was a total blast.

3. H.S. state basketball titles

The McPherson Bullpups won three straight state titles while I was the team's voice. Ex-ESPN SportsCenter Anchor and WWE star Jonathan Coachman was on one of those teams. Dude's vertical was worse than mine, but he sure could score.

4. My first college football TV broadcast

Eastern Washington at Sacramento State, 2003. Off the top of my head, Daniel Fells and Marco Cavka from that game both played in the NFL. So did a lineman from Sac State.

5. Being in the zone

It didn't happen often, but it happened at least once—McPherson College men's basketball at Southwestern College. I remember seeing match-ups so well that I anticipated the moves Mac coach Roger Trimmell would make before he made them.

6. Traveling

My sportscasting career took me places I might not have visited otherwise. Places like Pocatello and Des Moines were interesting because they were so different from my home turf in San Diego. However, Idaho's snow and Iowa's mosquitos the size of small Volkswagens were ultimately forgettable.

The best place I traveled to was Orlando, FL with the Piranhas. I mentioned it earlier. Add to that Disney World, running the stairs in the Orlando Arena with one of the assistant coaches and hitting the town with other members of the traveling party. Friends said there were beautiful women in Orlando, but I was too busy building my spotting boards to notice.

Traveling with the Piranhas was even more fun than calling the games. Visiting new places was one of the outstanding aspects of my sportscasting career.

The enjoyment of sports broadcasting comes as much from the people we meet and the places we visit as from the events we cover.

THE MOST MEMORABLE DAY IN MY SPORTSCASTING CAREER

When Jeanne Zelasko called me one morning in October 1993, I felt like my big break had finally arrived.

Three months earlier, I had moved back to my hometown of San Diego after three years of entry-level radio in McPherson, KS. For the final two of those three years, I had been trying unsuccessfully to get on board at XTRA Sports 690—just the second all-sports station in the country at the time.

Finally, I decided I must live in San Diego before an employer there would hire me. So I moved west, introduced myself to station Program Director Howard Freedman, and told him I was interested in future opportunities.

Jeanne Zelasko has enjoyed a fabulous sports broadcasting career—including as a longtime member of Fox Sports' Major League Baseball coverage. In the Fall of '93, though, she was XTRA's Morning Drive sports anchor and handled the scheduling of air talent.

Jeanne called me that October morning to tell me someone called in sick. She asked if I could do sports updates on legendary host Lee "Hacksaw" Hamilton's show that afternoon. It took me about half a second to say yes.

I put on a coat and tie that afternoon, went to the station, and had a flawless sports update shift. I remember Hacksaw sticking his head into the studio before at least two of my updates to remind me to "keep it short." It wasn't that I was going long; it was that less of me meant more of him. Saw liked that.

After my shift, I met my parents to celebrate at our favorite Chinese restaurant. They had listened to each of my sports updates. As we shared egg drop soup, broccoli beef, and sweet and sour pork, my parents' obvious excitement and pride in me made me feel like a million bucks.

It still does.

Overcome feelings of underappreciation

One of my coworkers at XTRA Sports 690 was a legend in the sports broadcasting industry. Chet Forte was the longtime director of Monday Night Football in the days of Howard Cosell, Frank Gifford, and Dandy Don Meredith. After Chet's well-publicized gambling problems forced him off the broadcasts, he got his life in order and returned to broadcasting as a sports talk host at our station.

Chet was great to all of us—kind, generous, and fun. I especially enjoyed attending the city high school basketball championships with him, then him treating me to dinner afterward at a nearby Black Angus steak house.

Chet passed away while still employed at XTRA. We all owed him a debt of gratitude and appreciation, and the entire staff wanted to attend his funeral to pay our respects and support his family.

Radio stations require 24/7 programming, even during a funeral. I volunteered to miss Chet's service and fill in for other hosts so they could attend. That day, I hosted the mid-morning show, hustled to Qualcomm Stadium to cover a Padres afternoon game, and then high-tailed it back to the station to host my night show. I was on the clock for roughly 12 hours that day, from midday to midnight.

My motivation was to help my team. However, in the immaturity of my youth, I also wanted to be thanked for my effort.

I never heard thank you from management or anyone for who I filled in. I felt underappreciated.

Here's why I bring it up: Most everyone in sportscasting at some point feels overworked, underappreciated, and underpaid. There are long hours. You wear a lot of hats. You don't earn what you think you deserve and rarely get a pat on the back.

How do you feel better about it?

Here's the key:

What you are not getting in appreciation and compensation, you are getting in an opportunity.

Your employer is paying you to build your resume and polish your craft in pursuit of your next job. They're paying you to prepare yourself for bigger and better opportunities.

Looking at it that way, you'll quickly stop feeling underappreciated and stay motivated.

HANDLING CRITICS

I couldn't have worked in sports broadcasting today. My skin is too thin.

Even if 99% of the internet comments about my talk show or play-by-play were excellent, I would dwell on the 1% that weren't. I would dwell on it to the point I would consider tweaking what I was doing to appease the 1%.

Big mistake. Don't be me. Be realistic. Be mentally strong.

Some things to consider about critics:

1. They're called critics for a reason.

There aren't as many newspaper critics as there used to be, but sports radio and TV critics still exist. Their job isn't to coddle. It's to criticize. It draws eyeballs. The fact they don't write good things about you doesn't mean you aren't doing good things.

2. It is primarily unhappy people who share opinions.

Folks who like something don't generally go out of their way to say so publicly. It is usually negative people who are critical online. Misery loves company. It makes no sense to give credibility to people like this.

3. The only person whose opinion counts is your employer's.

Your boss putting you on the air should be all the validation you need. They are trying to make money and think you can help them do it.

We all need feedback to improve, but be choosy about where you get it. Suggestions from industry professionals carry tremendous value. Something you read on social media from Sam in Sheboygan does not.

Here's a tip for handling your critics: Kill them with kindness when possible.

When I was working in San Diego, a weekly radio/TV critic wrote only negative comments about me when he wrote about me at all. One day, I stepped into the elevator at a Chargers game, and there he was. I took those 10 seconds to introduce myself and tell him how much I enjoyed his work. In his next column, he wrote something complimentary about me. He never wrote anything negative about me again.

And remember this: A lion doesn't concern himself with the opinions of sheep.

THE SILENT ENEMY: FEAR OF FAILURE

I was a weekend and fill-in host at XTRA Sports in 1995. I made a New Year's resolution to get a full-time sports talk gig within nine months.

Nine months passed, and I was still a weekend and fill-in host. (If a resolution fails, there is solace in having it fail in paradise.)

It was only through the wisdom of aging I realized years later why my resolution didn't come to fruition:

Fear of failure.

I gave maybe only 40% effort to make it become a reality. **I didn't go all-in because if I came up short, I would have felt like I failed**—like I wasn't good enough to achieve my dream of being a full-time host.

The 28-year-old me didn't understand that putting 100% effort towards my resolution would have left me much better off than I had been before.

I still would have won. Aim for perfection, and you'll capture greatness.

Don't let fear of failure stop you from going all-out in pursuit of your goals. The pursuit guarantees growth.

DON'T LET REGRET CREEP INTO YOUR SPORTSCASTING CAREER

I am jealous of Graham Bensinger.

Among journalists today, Bensinger is a giant among long-form interviewers—up to 30 or 60 minutes with a single guest. His interviews are intelligent, well-researched, and well-planned.

I envy Bensinger because I once wanted to be recognized as the king of interviewing. I hosted Weekend AllNight on ESPN Radio from 1999 to 2003. We'd spend two or three segments interviewing a single guest each Saturday. My goal was to ask questions the guests had never been asked. It kept them and my audience enthused and engaged.

Former Cal star QB and later head coach Joe Kapp was my guest one night. I asked Kapp who Mrs. So-and-So was. He gasped audibly. "She was my third-grade teacher. She had as profound an impact on me growing up as anyone." I knew that because of my research. Kapp went on to explain his teacher's influence. It was riveting.

Another time, my guest was one of the legendary Harlem Globetrotters. I found an old documentary on VHS tape in the local library while preparing. The show explained how the Trotters would "accidentally" misfire a pass into the lap of a hot woman in the audience. When my guest returned to the bench after retrieving the errant pass, a teammate asked if the visit was successful—if he "got the digits." On the air, I asked my guest what it meant when his teammate asked, "Did you get the digits?" He laughed uproariously for several seconds before asking how I knew about their trick for collecting phone numbers.

Once, I interviewed Al Oliver, who had won batting titles in both the American and National Leagues. In prepping, I discovered an incredible hot streak he once enjoyed—one that, to this day, has rarely been matched. I'll always remember his reply when I brought it up. "In all the years I've been interviewed, nobody has ever asked me about that, and it was one of the most memorable accomplishments of my career."

Interviewing, researching, and asking unique questions were things I loved. I loved listening for great follow-up opportunities. I loved leading my guests to tell stories.

Here's the point: I didn't love long-form interviewing enough to pursue it doggedly as Graham Bensinger did. **If you want something badly enough, you'll make it happen. Otherwise, you'll make an excuse.**

I first heard of Graham Bensinger when he was roughly 13 years old, tracking down big-name athletes and interviewing them on whatever platform he had. He's aggressively pursued it ever since. He did what I wasn't willing to do. I still feel regret.

YOU CAN DO IT!

When I visit college sportscasting classes, students most commonly ask me this question:

"What can I do to stand out in the sportscasting industry?"

My reply is simple: Become an elite person. The advice applies to young sportscasters and veterans alike. Remember, working on yourself is even more important than working on your career. Applying the tenets in this book will help you address both. Find something to improve in your personal or professional life every day. No improvement is too small. Just move forward daily. Be conscientious; continual growth will help you achieve your sportscasting goals.

A goal without a plan is only a dream. Let this book serve as your plan to help you achieve your sportscasting goals. You can do it.

Good luck!

Appendix

STAA Play-by-Play Pyramid

The building blocks of great play-by-play.

- **Time and score:** New listeners don't want to wait. At least every 90 seconds.
- **Pinpoint the ball**: Where exactly is the ball? Use both vertical and horizontal reference points.
- **Description:** Relevant action, movements, behaviors, sights, sounds, smells & emotions of players, coaches, fans and atmosphere.
- **Why does this matter?** Turns your broadcast into a story. Explain what's at stake in this game, this moment, this possession, this play, this at-bat.
- **Who is important?** Develops the characters (teams, players & coaches) in your story.
- **Recap:** Tell new listeners how the game got to this point. Every 8-10 minutes.
- **Voice as instrument:** Match your pacing to the speed of the action. Use inflections and pauses for emphasis and dramatic effect. Be appropriately energetic & excited but never scream.

STAA Sports Talk/Podcast Pyramid

The building blocks of great sports talk shows and podcasts.

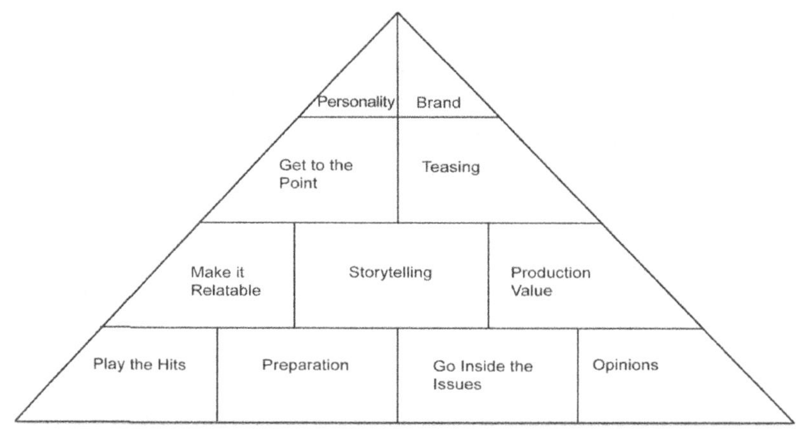

- **Play the hits:** Address stories that are of most interest to most of your audience.
- **Opinions:** Have them, research them, support them, defend them.
- **Preparation**: Support your opinions with facts.
- **Go inside the issues**: Tell your listeners what's new, what's next, and what is possible.
- **Make it relatable**: Give context to issues by drawing parallels to similar situations in other sports, pop culture, your personal life, etc.
- **Storytelling:** Drive your point home by sharing first-hand experience & observation. Give listeners something they can't get anywhere else. Every segment should include at least one story.
- **Production value:** Use audio elements to enhance your spoken presentation.
- **Get to the point**: Grab listeners within the first 30 seconds of each segment.
- **Teasing:** Build Time Spent Listening (TSL) by enticing listeners to listen longer or tune in later.
- **Personality**: Be one. Traits might include being genuine, opinionated, self-deprecating, insightful, thought-provoking, observant, curious, witty, and well-rounded.
- **Branding:** Repeat the name of your show and station call letters. It's advertising.

Resume Rubric

Give yourself the number of points listed next to their corresponding features. Add your total then compare it to the scale to see how your resume rates.

(5) Your resume isn't boring black and white. It sizzles with color, icons, graphics, and your headshot.

(4) One page

(3) Employment from more than 10 years ago is excluded

(3) Uses bullet points

(3) The experience section is listed first

(2) Your name is the largest font on the page

(2) Header features a link to your online demo and resume

(2) There is no objective

(2) There is no space-wasting summary

(2) It excludes references in favor of fun facts about yourself

(2) Bold and underlined text is used only for section headings

(1) All four margins are at least 0.75 inches

(1) There are blank lines between sections. (White space is your friend)

(1) Header includes city and state but no street address

______Total Score

How does your resume rate?

30-33 Your resume is helping you in the job market. Well done!

23-29 Your resume needs work.

0-22 Your resume is doing more harm than good.

Cover Letter Rubric

Give yourself the number of points listed next to their corresponding features. Add your total then compare it to the scale to see how your cover letter rates.

(4) Zero typos

(4) The spelling of the employer's name and gender has been double-checked

(3) Specific statement of why this employer interests you more than others

(3) Features only your relevant experience

(3) Two-thirds of a page, maximum

(3) Does not repeat your resume

(2) The opening paragraph includes a statement of interest

(2) Excludes phrases like "dream job" and "it would be an honor"

(2) Focuses on what you can do for the employer, not what they can do for you

(2) Includes words and phrases from the position description

(2) Includes a date upon which you will follow up

(2) Omits self-evaluations

(1) Avoids "I" more than twice in any paragraph

(1) Avoids "I believe," "I think," and "I feel"

(1) Excludes repetitive words or phrase

(1) Includes a reference

_____ **Total Score**

How does your cover letter rate?

29-36 You're making a great first impression!

22-28 You can do better.

0-21 Your cover letter is weak enough that employers are unlikely to review your demo.

Acknowledgements

Expressions of gratitude must start with my parents Dave and Suzanne, sister Debbie, wife Amy, and son Ryan. Their support of me is unwavering, and their love smooths life's rough spots. My happiest times are in their company. And Dupe (Ryan)—you make me proud, and you make me happy, every single day.

Second, much appreciation goes to the people who have helped build Sportscasters Talent Agency of America. Most of the great ideas in the company's formative years and their execution are attributable to Melodie Turori. I'm not too smart. I am smart enough, though, to surround myself with people who are smarter than me. I'm forever indebted, Mel. My deepest thanks also go to Jordan Carruth, Brendan Gulick, and Michael Wottreng. Each of you has made STAA better. Michael, thank you especially for being patient when I make suggestions for things I know nothing about. My wife Amy is due additional thanks here, too. A new wave of growth occurred when she offered to take several time-consuming responsibilities off my plate.

Thank you to the more than 3,000 people who have been STAA members since 2006. Each of you has trusted us to help you advance your career. We take that responsibility seriously. The number of folks who bet on us early on, when we had no track record, was humbling and cool. We will always work hard to justify the trust of our members.

Many people helped with the creation of this book. And guess what—it starts yet again with Amy. She planted the idea at least a dozen years before I thought I could pull it off. She's always believed in me before I believed in myself. She has a master's degree, and now I have a book.

More thanks to Amy and to Troy Powers. Their thoughtful edits strengthened every chapter. The book I would have put out into the world would have been silly without their sharp minds and eyes. I'm grateful for their insight, time, and belief in this project.

Thank you to Shawn Parker and Tim Clagg for permission to include their cool-looking resumes in the book.

Additional gratitude goes to friends Mike Capps, Mario Impemba, John Leahy, Kevin Long, Bill Rogan, and Josh Suchon. All are published authors who provided invaluable guidance about how to publish a book. And to my friend Dan Graves, who gave me the courage to start my own business.

Last but certainly not least, thank YOU. I'll reference trust again. Thank you for trusting this book would be worth your investment of time and money. Hopefully, you're already applying new career-building strategies and seeing results from your efforts.

Here's to you and your sportscasting success. Go be great!

About STAA

Sportscasters Talent Agency of America (STAA; staatalent.com) is a membership service owned by former ESPN Radio talk show host Jon Chelesnik. STAA helps sportscasters advance their careers. Members learn where job openings are and receive step-by-step advice about how to stand out when applying. Members also connect with like-minded sportscasters and improve their craft.

In addition to the paid membership, STAA provides a variety of free resources to assist you:

The public **STAA job board** has been a go-to for the industry since 2006. It features a comprehensive list of sports broadcasting opportunities, from major college play-by-play to podcasting and TV sports anchor/reporter positions. Best of all, it's free!

The **STAA blog** includes inspiring stories and strategies to help you advance your career.

The **Resources** section of the STAA website offers curated tools and guidance for sportscasters at different stages of their careers.

STAA's **YouTube channel** features how-to videos to help you move forward in your career, plus interviews with top sportscasters and employers to motivate and help you improve your craft.

Check out some of our notable alumni:

https://staatalent.com/notable-alumni

About the Author

JON CHELESNIK is the founder and owner of Sportscasters Talent Agency of America. When he realized the NBA had no interest in slow guards who can't shoot, he decided broadcasting sports was the next best career option. Play-by-play in McPherson, KS, and sports radio and TV in San Diego led to four years of hosting on ESPN Radio Network.

Eventually, Jon started helping other sportscasters build their careers. He began asking employers what they look for when hiring talent. He hasn't stopped asking since.

Sometimes, Jon misses being on air. However, being home in San Diego at night and on weekends with his wife Amy and son Ryan is worth the trade-off. They love reading, playing board games, and going to the beach together. Jon also binges on Friday Night Lights reruns. He believes FNL and Leave it to Beaver are the best shows ever produced.

To learn more about Jon, visit:

https://staatalent.com/about

Made in the USA
Coppell, TX
24 February 2026